Remember This?

People, Things and Events
FROM **1962** TO THE **PRESENT DAY**

UK EDITION

With thanks for additional research by Dale Barham, Nicola Gardiner
and Janice Morton.

Baby names: Office of National Statistics.

Cover images: Mary Evans - Keystone Pictures USA/zumapress.com,
Marx Memorial Library, London Fire Brigade, The Watts Collection.
Cover icons from rawpixel/Freepik.

Cover Design: Fanni Williams / thehappycolourstudio.com

The Milestone Memories series including this *Remember This?*
title is produced by Milestones Memories Press, a division
of Say So Media Ltd.

First edition: October 2021

We've tried our best to check our facts, but mistakes can still slip through.
Spotted one? We'd love to know about it: info@saysomedia.net

Rewind, Replay, Remember

What can you remember before you turned six? If you're like most of us, not much: the comforting smell of a blanket or the rough texture of a sweater, perhaps. A mental snapshot of a parent arriving home late at night. A tingle of delight or the shadow of sorrow.

But as we grow out of childhood, our autobiographical and episodic memories – they're the ones hitched to significant events such as birthdays or leaving school – are created and filed more effectively, enabling us to piece them together at a later date. And the more we revisit those memories, the less likely we are to lose the key that unlocks them.

These fragments are assembled into a more-or-less coherent account of our lives – the one we tell ourselves, our friends, our relatives. And while this one-of-a-kind biopic loses a little definition over the years, some episodes remain in glorious technicolour – although it's often the most embarrassing incidents!

But this is one movie that's never quite complete. Have you ever had a memory spring back unbidden, triggered by something seemingly unrelated? This book is an attempt to discover those forgotten scenes using the events, sounds, and faces linked to the milestones in your life.

It's time to blow off the cobwebs and see how much you can remember!

It Happened in 1962

The biggest event in the year is one that didn't make the front pages: you were born! Here are some of the national stories that people were talking about.

- ✦ The Sunday Times first newspaper to print colour supplement
- ✦ BBC's satirical show That Was The Week That Was first aired
- ✦ New Coventry Cathedral consecrated
- ✦ BBC broadcasts first episode of police drama Z-Cars
- ✦ Family saloon the Ford Cortina goes on sale for £573
- ✦ Chris Bonington becomes first Briton to climb Eiger's north face
- ✦ James Hanratty hanged for A6 murder despite doubts over guilt
- ✦ First Bond film Dr No, starring Sean Connery, hits UK cinemas
- ✦ Safeway opens its first supermarket in Bedford
- ✦ Watson, Crick and Wilkins win Nobel Prize for work on DNA
- ✦ The Beatles release first single Love Me Do
- ✦ Golden Wonder launches its first flavoured crisp – Cheese & Onion
- ✦ Rudolf Nureyev and Margot Fonteyn debut together in Giselle
- ✦ London's electric trolley buses phased out
- ✦ Britain hit by Boxing Day Big Freeze that lasts until April
- ✦ First passenger hovercraft service launched on north Wales coast (right)
- ✦ Push-button Panda road crossings introduced
- ✦ Smallpox outbreak in Cardiff – 900,000 vaccinated
- ✦ IRA calls off Border Campaign in Northern Ireland
- ✦ Education Act sees state funding of university tuition fees
- ✦ BBC broadcasts first episode of sitcom Steptoe and Son

Born this year:
- ☜ Snooker ace Jimmy 'Whirlwind' White born in Balham, London
- ☜ Actor Ralph Nathaniel Twisleton-Wykeham-Fiennes born in Ipswich
- ☜ TV and radio presenter Vanessa Feltz born in north London

Six times a day, this pioneering passenger service – dubbed a 'hovercoach' because hovercraft was trademarked – plied between Wallasey and Rhyl at nearly 70mph in 1962. By the eighties, hovercraft ferried millions of passengers and cars across the Channel. But fuel price rises, the noise and the advent of catamaran engineering prompted the decline of the 'flying crab'. Just one commercial scheduled service remains, across the Solent

On the Bookshelf When You Were Small

The books of our childhood linger long in the memory. These are the children's classics, all published in your first ten years. Do you remember the stories? What about the covers?

1962	Wolves of Willoughby Chase by Joan Aiken
1963	The Secret Passage by Nina Bawden
1963	Stig of the Dump by Clive King
1963	Where the Wild Things Are by Maurice Sendak
1964	On the Run by Nina Bawden
1964	Flat Stanley by Jeff Brown
1964	Charlie and the Chocolate Factory by Roald Dahl
1964	**Chitty-Chitty-Bang-Bang by Ian Fleming** It was adapted for film four years after Fleming's death – produced by Albert R Broccoli, co-written by Roald Dahl.
1965	Over Sea, Under Stone by Susan Cooper
1966	The Witch's Daughter by Nina Bawden
1966	**The Magic Finger by Roald Dahl** Originally titled The Almost Ducks, publication in the US was delayed over fears of offending the gun lobby.
1967	The Owl Service by Alan Garner
1967	Brown Bear, What Do You See? by Bill Martin Jr
1968	The Wombles by Elisabeth Beresford
1968	The Whispering Mountain by Joan Aiken
1968	The Iron Man by Ted Hughes
1968	The Tiger Who Came to Tea by Judith Kerr
1968	Elmer the Elephant by David McKee
1968	The Pigman by Paul Zindel
1969	**The Very Hungry Caterpillar by Eric Carle** Began life as A Week With Willi the Worm, the story of a bookworm, but Carle's publisher requested a caterpillar.
1970	**Are You There, God? It's Me, Margaret by Judy Blume** Challenged and banned due to the discussion of menstruation, puberty, pornography, and religion.
1970	Fantastic Mr Fox by Roald Dahl
1971	Mr. Tickle by Roger Hargreaves

Around the World in Your Birth Year

Here are the events from abroad that were big enough to make news at home in the year you were born. And you won't remember any of them!

- Algeria gains independence from France
- Pop artist Andy Warhol's Campbell's Soup works go on show
- Oscar-winning epic Lawrence of Arabia released
- First Walmart store opens in Rogers, Arkansas
- Superhero Spider-Man first appears in Marvel comic
- Jawaharlal Nehru becomes prime minister of India for fourth time
- Brazil beats Czechoslovakia to win World Cup in Santiago, Chile
- The Rolling Stones make their debut at London's Marquee Club
- European ferry firm Stena Line founded in Gothenburg, Sweden
- Astronaut John Glenn becomes first American to orbit Earth
- 130 killed in take-off crash at Paris Orly Airport
- Former Belgian colony Rwanda becomes independent
- US-USSR standoff over Soviet nuclear missiles in Cuba ends
- Three escape US prison Alcatraz using spoons and homemade raft
- Dutch electronics firm Philips produces first audio cassette
- Mount Huascaran landslide in Peru claims 4,000 lives
- Nelson Mandela jailed for incitement to rebellion in South Africa
- Troubled star Marilyn Monroe dies of drug overdose in LA
- New York gang musical West Side Story wins 10 Oscars

Born this year:
- Canadian actor Jim Carrey born in Newmarket, Ontario
- Rapper MC Hammer born Stanley Kirk Burrell in Oakland, California
- Australian filmmaker Mark Anthony 'Baz' Luhrmann born in Sydney
- US actress Alicia Christian 'Jodie' Foster born in Los Angeles

Boys' Names When You Were Born

Stuck for a name in the early 20th century? The answer was simple: use your own. Will nobody think of the genealogists? Here are the most popular names in England and Wales in 1962.

David
David has wrestled control of the top spot from John, and he'll keep it for twenty years.

John
Stephen
Michael
Peter
Robert
Paul
Alan
Christopher
Richard
Anthony
Andrew
Ian
James
William
Philip
Brian
Keith
Graham

Rising and falling stars:
Farewell Bernard, Frank, Norman, Leonard, Lawrence and Clifford. Give a big Top 100 welcome to Jeremy, Julian and all the G's: Gerard, Garry, Gareth and Gregory and Glenn.

A note about other parts of the UK:
Baby name data isn't available until 1974 for Scotland and the turn of the century for Northern Ireland. How different are they? In the mid-seventies around a third of Scotland's Top 100 boys' names weren't in the English and Welsh equivalent – but the highest ranked of these was Gordon at number 30. By 2019, Scotland-only names ranked 4th (Harris), 7th (Lewis), 18th (Brodie), 22nd (Finlay) and more.

Girls' Names When You Were Born

Some parents pick names that are already popular. Others try to pick something more unusual – only to find out a few years later that thousands had the same idea.

Susan
After thirty years, Susan takes the top spot from Margaret.

Linda
Christine
Margaret
Janet
Patricia
Carol
Elizabeth
Mary
Anne
Ann
Jane
Jacqueline
Barbara
Sandra
Gillian
Pauline
Elaine
Lesley
Angela
Pamela
Helen
Jennifer
Valerie

Jean
Slides from the Top 100 are usually gentle. But not for Jean: by the sixties, she was gone.

Rising and falling stars:
A quarter of names in this Top 100 haven't been seen since, including Rita, Geraldine and Doreen. Taking their place are names such as Gail, Dawn, Anna, Fiona and Beverley.

Things People Did When You Were Growing Up...

...that hardly anyone does now. Some of these we remember fondly; others are best left in the past!

+ Use a mangle
+ **Use an outside toilet**
  Slum clearances and grants saw the end of most outside toilets, although in 2010 around 40,000 properties still had one.

+ Take the trolley bus to school
+ Fetch coal from the cellar
+ Wear a hat to work
+ **Use a coal tar vaporizer**
  A coal tar inhaler or vaporizer - probably made by Wright's, with the matching liquid - seemed like a good idea for treating whooping cough. It wasn't. A 1930s example held by the National Trust has a simple caption: 'This is poisonous.'

+ Travel without a seatbelt
+ **Rent a TV**
  When tellies cost a fortune (and frequently broke), renting a TV made sense. Where to go? Radio Rentals, who promised, 'You'll be glued to our sets, not stuck with them!'

+ **Wear a housecoat**
  Who can think of a housecoat and curlers without remembering Coronation Street's Hilda Ogden?

+ Scrub your doorstep
+ Creosote the fence (banned for DIY in 2003)
+ **Smoke a pipe**
  Stephen Fry was the last Pipe Smoker of the Year, in 2003.

+ **Spank (or be spanked)**
  Corporal punishment ended in most schools in 1986. It is illegal in Scottish and Welsh homes, but not in England or N. Ireland.

+ Pay the Pools collector
+ Build a soapcart
+ **Write a letter**
  Royal Mail still handles 10 billion letters each year but very few are handwritten. More than a fifth of UK children have never received a letter.

Old-fashioned Games

In a pre-digital age, boardgames ruled. Many of these predate you buy decades, centuries or more but still played; others gather dust in attics and charity shops.

1928	Escalado
1934	Sorry!
1935	**Monopoly**

Monopoly
The origins of this stalwart lie with The Landlord's Game, an education tool patented in 1904 by Elizabeth Magie. (The anti-monopoly version - Prosperity - didn't catch on.) It was the first game to feature a never-ending path rather than a fixed start and finish.

1938	Buccaneer
1938	Scrabble
1935	Whot!
1947	Subbuteo
1949	**Cluedo**

Cluedo
Cluedo, or Clue as it is known in the USA, introduced us to a host of shady country house characters and a selection of murder weapons. For years those included a piece of genuine lead pipe - thankfully replaced on health grounds.

1925	Dover Patrol
1851	**Happy Families**

Happy Families
The original and much-copied Happy Families card game was launched for the Great Exhibition in 1851. For 20th Century children, Happy Families also means the million-selling book series by Allan Ahlberg, based loosely on the card game, which in turn inspired a BBC series.

1889	**Tiddlywinks**

Tiddlywinks
Trademarked as Tiddledy-Winks by Joseph Fincher, this much-maligned game has nevertheless found fans at elite universities, spawned countless spin-offs and rule variations (known in Tiddlywink parlance as 'perversions').

1896	Ludo
1892	Chinese Chequers
1938	Totopoly
Ancient Egypt	Mancala

Things People Do Now...

...that were virtually unknown when you were young.
How many of these habits are part of your routine or even
second nature these days? Do you remember the first time?

- ✦ Shop on Sunday (made possible in England and Wales in 1994)
- ✦ Microwave a curry
- ✦ **Leave a voicemail**
  At least you'll never have to change the cassette again!
- ✦ **Watch last night's TV**
  Nowadays, you don't have to remember to set the VCR (and get a
  small child to help you do it). BBC iPlayer was the UK's first
  on-demand, streaming service, launched in 2007.

- ✦ Strim grass
- ✦ Change a fitted sheet
- ✦ Recharge your toothbrush
- ✦ Order a takeaway meal... to be delivered
- ✦ Delete a photo
- ✦ **Fit a disposable nappy**
  The first disposable 'napkins' went on sale in 1949 as two-part
  Paddis, invented by Valerie Hunter Gordon.

- ✦ Eat an avocado
- ✦ Use Google
- ✦ Take a shower
- ✦ **Make a video call (right)**
- ✦ Buy a cheap flight
- ✦ **Floss your teeth**
  Not a flosser? Take heart from a 2016 US research review:
  evidence for its benefit is very weak, and official advice to floss
  was dropped. Poking around with those pesky interdental
  brushes is how you should be spending your time (and money).

- ✦ Pressure wash your patio
- ✦ **Stick a self-adhesive stamp**
  You can probably still remember the taste of stamp glue, even
  though the sticky versions were introduced in 1993.

- ✦ Answer an email (or send it to spam)
- ✦ **Use a duvet**
  Sir Terence Conran is credited with finally persuading Brits to
  ditch the blankets when he introduced duvets in his Habitat
  stores in the sixties.

Zoom, Skype, FaceTime and more: if you weren't making face-to-face calls before the lockdowns of 2020, that's probably when you made your first. But it has taken 50 years to catch on and for technology to catch up: shown above is AT&T's PicturePhone, demonstrated in 1964 at New York's World's Fair. (The cost didn't help: renting a pair of devices for three minutes cost the equivalent of £100.)

Popular Food from the 1950s

Rationing was thankfully over (it ended in 1954). But fifties food was probably still on the menu when you were small. Tins of everything, stacked high. For flavour, take your pick: ketchup, brown sauce, or salad cream. Olive oil? It's still in the bathroom cabinet. Still, some dishes were worth keeping: who can resist a coronation chicken sandwich?

Milkshakes
Thick, creamy and an ideal hiding place for a lethal dose of poison. That's what the CIA thought when they plotted to slip a pill into Castro's beloved chocolate milkshake. Fortunately for the Cuban leader, the pill stuck to the freezer door.

Chop Suey

Real cream cakes

Bananas
In the 1950s, Gros Michel bananas - the dominant banana sold - were wiped out by the Panama disease, nearly destroying the banana industry.

Peaches

Frosties
Introduced in 1954 as Sugar Frosted Flakes, this new cereal was an instant hit - as was Tony the Tiger.

Frozen chicken

Tinned pineapple
Think pineapple, think Hawaii. Pineapples are still cultivated there, although the state's last cannery closed in 2006.

Spam fritters
Dubbed the 'Miracle Meat' when it was introduced in the late thirties, Spam is no longer made in the UK but it's still popular. Worldwide, around 7 billion cans have been sold; 44,000 cans are still produced every hour.

Baked Alaska

Devilled eggs

Coronation chicken

Hamburgers
In the US during WWII, hamburgers were briefly rebranded 'liberty steaks' in a renewed bout of food-as-propaganda. In World War I, sauerkraut was 'liberty cabbage' while French fries became 'freedom fries' during the Iraq war.

Pre-war Chocolate

Many of the chocolate bars we enjoy today were dreamed up long before WWII – though recipes, sizes and names have mostly been given a tweak or two over the decades to keep them as our newsagent favourites.

800s	**Fry's Chocolate Cream** The first chocolate bars to be mass-produced.
905	Cadbury Dairy Milk
908	Bourneville
914	Fry's Turkish Delight
920	Flake
926	Cadbury's Fruit & Nut
927	**Jaffa Cake** Her Majesty's Customs and Excise tried to argue that a Jaffa Cake is a biscuit and subject to VAT. McVitie's won the day, in part because Jaffa cakes go hard when stale, unlike biscuits which go soft.
929	Crunchie
932	**Mars Bar** Want to buy a Mars bar in the US? Ask for a Milky Way.
932	Penguin
935	Aero
935	**Milky Way** The Milky Way is not named after our galaxy, but instead after a type of malted milk, or milkshake as it's now known.
936	Milky Bar
937	**Kit Kat** Before Joseph Rowntree trademarked the term 'Kit Kat' in 1911 and the snack's eventual launch in the thirties, the name was most commonly associated with a mutton pie made by pastry chef Christopher Catt. He served it in his London Kit-Cat Club during the late 17th Century.
937	Rolo
939	**Marathon** In 1990, Marathon became Snickers: the US name since its 1930 launch (named after Frank Mars's horse). In the seventies, Mars sold a chocolate bar in the US called the Marathon – and it's still on sale here as the Curly Wurly.

Cars of your Childhood (Pt.1)

These are the cars that first hit the streets in the decade before you were born. Only one in five households had a car by 1960 and as cars became more reliable and popular, so the number buying second-hand grew, too. So if you travelled by car as a child, there's a strong possibility you were cooped up in one of these fifties favourites.

Austin Westminster

Ford Prefect
In The Hitchhiker's Guide to the Galaxy, an arriving alien picks the name Ford Prefect thinking it would be inconspicuous.

Vauxhall Velox

Sunbeam Talbot

Rover 60

Ford Anglia
Features on the cover of Harry Potter and the Chamber of Secrets.

Ford Consul

Hillman Minx

Morris Minor
Originally named Mosquito, the name was changed at the last minute as it was feared that the name would deter conservative buyers. It went on to become the first million-selling British car.

MG Magnette

Morris Oxford

Standard Vanguard
Named after a Navy battleship to appeal to ex-servicemen.

Austin Cambridge

Wolseley / Riley One Point Five
The Riley One Point Five and the Wolseley shared features including the engine, suspension and dimensions. The Riley was originally intended as a replacement for the Morris Minor.

Ford Popular

Land Rover
The first Land Rover was inspired by World War II jeeps, with the steering wheel in the middle. A Land Rover with tank tracks for agricultural work and a monster truck version followed.

Austin A30
Dubbed the steel teddy bear due to its rounded, cute appearance.

The close of the decade before you were born brought a rather less welcome motoring innovation: the parking meter. The first meters installed in 1958 in Mayfair, London (sixpence for an hour, a shilling for two), triggered the predictable result from day one: parked cars crammed onto neighbouring streets without restrictions, below.

The Biggest Hits When You Were 10

Whistled by your father, hummed by your sister or overheard on the radio, these are the hit records as you reached double digits.

Telegram Sam ♪ T Rex
Son of My Father ♪ Chicory Tip
Without You ♪ Nilsson
Amazing Grace ♪ Royal Scots Dragoon Guards
Metal Guru ♪ T Rex
Vincent ♪ Don McLean
Don McLean's timeless classic Vincent was inspired by
Vincent Van Gogh's painting, The Starry Night.

Take Me Bak 'Ome ♪ Slade
Puppy Love ♪ Donny Osmond
Donny Osmond featured in a cartoon cameo in the children's
television show, Johnny Bravo.

School's Out ♪ Alice Cooper
The album cover for School's Out opens like a school desk
(you can see the original in the Hard Rock cafe in Las Vegas).
The original vinyl was wrapped in a pair of paper knickers.

You Wear It Well ♪ Rod Stewart
How Can I Be Sure ♪ David Cassidy
Mouldy Old Dough ♪ Lieutenant Pigeon
My Ding-a-Ling ♪ Chuck Berry
Chuck Berry may have helped invent rock'n'roll, but this is
the only number one of his entire career.

Tech Breakthroughs Before You Turned 25

Much of the technology we use today stands on the shoulders of the inventions made while you were small. Here are some of the most notable advances.

1962	Red LEDs
1965	Hypertext (http)
1966	Computer RAM
1967	**Hand-held calculator**

Hand-held, maybe: pocket-sized, definitely not. That came along in 1972 thanks to Clive Sinclair and his slimline Executive model – just one invention in his phenomenally productive career.

1967	**Computer mouse**

Doug Engelbart patented an early version of his 'X-Y indicator' in 1967. By the time a (very large) mouse became available with a Xerox computer in 1981, the patent had expired.

1969	Laser printer
1971	Email
1973	Mobile phone
1976	Apple Computer
1979	Barcodes
1979	Compact disc
1982	**Emoticons**

The inventor of the smiley emoticon hands out 'Smiley' cookies every Sept 19th – the anniversary of its first use.

1983	Internet
1983	Microsoft Word
1984	LCD projector
1984	Apple Macintosh
1985	**Sinclair C5**

Despite a body and a chassis designed by Lotus and assembled by Hoover, the ahead-of-its-time Sinclair C5 was plagued with problems including poor battery life, the inability to climb gentle hills and safety concerns.

On the Silver Screen When You Were 11

From family favourites to the films you weren't allowed to watch, these are the movies that dre the praise and crowds when you turned 11.

Save the Tiger 🎞 Jack Lemmon, Jack Gilford
Paper Moon 🎞 Ryan O'Neal, Tatum O'Neal
American Graffiti 🎞 Richard Dreyfuss, Ron Howard
Papillon 🎞 Steve McQueen, Dustin Hoffman
Westworld 🎞 Yul Brynner, Richard Benjamin
Carry On Girls 🎞 Sidney James, Barbara Windsor
The Wicker Man 🎞 Edward Woodward, Christopher Lee
High Plains Drifter 🎞 Clint Eastwood, Marianna Hill
The Sting 🎞 Paul Newman, Robert Redford
Father Dear Father 🎞 Patrick Cargill, Noel Dyson
Live and Let Die 🎞 Roger Moore, Jane Seymour
Moore's first outing as Bond.

The Way We Were 🎞 Barbra Streisand, Robert Redford
The Exorcist 🎞 Ellen Burstyn, Linda Blair
The Exorcist was reportedly so terrifying, audience members
fainted and left the cinema shaking and crying.

The Day of the Jackal 🎞 Edward Fox, Michael Lonsdale
The Hireling 🎞 Robert Shaw, Sarah Miles
Don't Look Now 🎞 Julie Christie, Donald Sutherland
Fans wondered: did Sutherland and Christie make love on
camera? So did Warren Beatty (Christie's boyfriend), who flew
across the world and threatened to have the film killed.

That'll Be the Day 🎞 David Essex, Rosemary Leach
A Touch of Class 🎞 George Segal, Glenda Jackson
Soylent Green 🎞 Charlton Heston, Leigh Taylor-Young
O Lucky Man! 🎞 Malcolm McDowell, Helen Mirren
Serpico 🎞 Al Pacino, Cornelia Sharpe
Serpico was shot in reverse order. Pacino started with his wild
hair and beard, then gradually shaved it during production so he
could reflect the clean-cut officer we meet at the start.

The Three Musketeers 🎞 Oliver Reed, Raquel Welch

Comics When You Were Small

Did you spend your childhood hopping from one foot to the other, longing for the next edition of your favourite comic to appear on the shelves? If so, these may be the titles you were waiting for.

Knockout ✳ (1939-1963)
Knockout Comics (or Knock-Out as they were originally known) ran for 24 years before merging into Valiant. However, you may remember it from its 1971 revival (without the hyphen!). Unlike most comics of the early 70s, every page was in colour.

Boys Own ✳ (1879-1967)
Twinkle ✳ (1968-1999)
The Eagle ✳ (1950-1969)
Robin ✳ (1953-1969)
Some of the most popular Robin comic strips included BBC children's characters Andy Pandy and the Flower Pot Men.

The Hornet ✳ (1963-1976)
Look And Learn ✳ (1962-1982)
The first issue of Look and Learn featured a photograph of a very young Prince Charles on the front cover.

TV Comic ✳ (1951-1984)
Jack and Jill ✳ (1954-1985)
Tiger ✳ (1954-1985)
The Topper ✳ (1953-1990)
Whizzer And Chips ✳ (1969-1990)
Jackie ✳ (1964-1993)
The Beezer ✳ (1956-1993)
For the first 25 years of its run, Beezer – companion to Topper – was printed in large-format A3.

Buster ✳ (1960-2000)
Bunty ✳ (1958-2001)
The Dandy ✳ (1937-2012)
Beano ✳ (1938-present)
The most valuable copies of the first issue of Beano fetch over £17,000 at auction. There are only 20 left in the world today.

Around the UK

Double digits at last: you're old enough to eavesdrop on adults and scan the headlines. These may be some of the earliest national news stories you remember.

- BBC quiz show Mastermind screened for first time
- IRA car bomb kills seven at Aldershot barracks
- Duke of Windsor, formerly King Edward VIII, dies in Paris
- Bloody Sunday – UK troops kill 14 on Derry civil-rights march
- Second Cod War begins as Iceland declares 50-mile exclusion zone
- UK far-left group The Angry Brigade go on trial for bombings
- British direct rule imposed; Northern Irish parliament suspended
- SAS parachutes into Atlantic to deal with QE2 bomb threat
- Thousands join CND four-day march to Aldermaston
- Long-running ITV soap Emmerdale broadcast for first time
- Luxury electric train Brighton Belle makes last trip from London
- UK unemployment tops one million
- School leaving age raised from 15 to 16
- Staines air crash kills all 118 onboard
- UK's last UK trolleybus makes final journey in Bradford
- Coal miners accept pay offer after seven-week strike
- First official UK Gay Pride rally held in London
- Deported Ugandan Asians start to arrive in UK
- Rock opera Jesus Christ Superstar opens in London's West End
- First official England-Scotland women's football match played
- Rose Heilbron first female judge to sit at Old Bailey

Born this year:
- Ginger Spice Geri Halliwell born in Watford
- Olympic gold-medallist rower James Cracknell born in Sutton, Surrey
- Actor and DJ Idris Elba born in Hackney, London

UK Buildings

Some were loathed then, loved now; others, the reverse. Some broke new architectural ground, others helped to power a nation or entertain. All of them were built before you were 40.

1962	Coventry Cathedral
1963	Bankside Power Station
1964	**Post Office Tower** The tower was previously a designated secret under the Official Secrets Act and didn't appear on any OS maps. It was a pretty prominent secret, though, and was used as a filming location for TV and film during this time.
1966	**Centre Point** One of London's first skyscrapers, 24-storey Centre Point was a lightning rod for those protesting the plight of the homeless. Built speculatively, it stood empty until the mid seventies, awaiting a tenant with deep pockets. The homeless charity Centrepoint uses its emblematic name.
1966	**Severn Bridge** Grade I listed, and since 2018, free to cross (both ways!).
1967	Queen Elizabeth Hall
1974	**Birmingham Library** Looked like 'a place where books are incinerated, not kept' said Prince Charles. It was demolished in 2013.
1976	National Exhibition Centre (NEC)
1976	**Brent Cross Centre** The UK's first American-style indoor shopping centre. The car park was used for the James Bond film Tomorrow Never Dies.
1980	NatWest Tower
1982	Barbican Centre
1986	Lloyd's Building
1991	**One Canada Square, London** This Canary Wharf icon spent 20 years as the UK's tallest building before The Shard stole its thunder.
2004	**30 St Mary Axe (The Gherkin), London** During construction, the remains of a Roman teenage girl were found buried on the site.
2012	The Shard, London

Early Radio 1 DJs

Do you remember the first time you heard 'the exciting new sound of Radio 1'? Replacing the BBC Light Programme in 1967, it soon won over the UK's youth to become the world's most popular station, and the DJs – all men until Annie Nightingale joined in 1970 – became household names.

Tony Blackburn
The man who started it all with those immortal words and span the first disc (Flowers in the Rain, by The Move). And don't forget his canine co-presenter, Arnold.

John Peel
Peel's life-long service to music is well known. But before this took off, his aspiration to be a journalist while selling insurance in Texas led him to bluff his way into the midnight news conference where Lee Harvey Oswald was paraded before the press.

Keith Skues

Ed Stewart
For children of the seventies, Ed Stewart means Crackerjack; but for those of us born earlier, it was Junior Choice on Saturday mornings where we'd get to know 'Stewpot'.

Mike Raven

Jimmy Young

Dave Cash

Kenny Everett
Everett was a Radio 1 DJ for less than three years before being sacked. He also appeared in 1980 on Just a Minute and was given the subject of marbles. Nicholas Parsons let him talk (while hesitating, repeating *and* deviating) for 90 seconds as a joke – assisted by the other panellists. He wasn't on the show again.

Terry Wogan

Duncan Johnson

Tommy Vance

Emperor Rosko
'Your groovy host from the West coast, here to clear up your skin and mess up your mind. It'll make you feel good all over!' – Rosko, aka Mike Pasternak, introducing his Midday Spin show.

Pete Murray

Bob Holness

Female Wimbledon Winners

Aged 15 in 1887, Lottie Dod was the youngest to win Wimbledon. Aged 37 in 1908, Charlotte Cooper Sterry was the oldest. These are the winners when you too were still in with a (slim) chance! Men, PTO!

977	**Virginia Wade** Wade competed at Wimbledon 15 times before winning. It was to be Britain's last female grand slam victory until Emma Raducanu's epic US Open win in 2021.
978-79	Martina Navratilova
980	Evonne Goolagong Cawley
981	**Chris Evert Lloyd** Nicknamed the Ice Maiden, Evert was the first tennis player to win 1,000 matches and the first female tennis player to reach $1 million in career prize money.
982-87	Martina Navratilova
988-89	Steffi Graf
990	Martina Navratilova
991-93	Steffi Graf
994	Conchita Martínez
995-96	Steffi Graf
997	**Martina Hingis** Hingis' mother had tennis dreams for her daughter before she was born; she named her after Martina Navratilova. Hingis was playing tennis by age two and at 12 years old, she became the youngest player to win a major junior title.
998	Jana Novotná
999	Lindsay Davenport

Wimbledon: The Men

In the men's tournament, Becker won at the tender age of 17. At the top end, Federer won in 2017 at the age of 35. But in 1909, in the amateur era, Arthur Gore was a nimble 41 years young – giving us our 'winning window' of 17 to 41.

1976-80	**Björn Borg** Sweden's Ice Man dominated the late seventies with his unusual baseline play, incredible fitness and good looks. Retirement at the age of 26 didn't suit him and at 34 he attempted a no-practice comeback with the same wooden racket (everyone else by then was using graphite). Unsurprisingly, it didn't pan out – unlike his revitalised and highly successful fashion label.
1981	John McEnroe
1982	Jimmy Connors
1983-84	John McEnroe
1985-86	Boris Becker
1987	Pat Cash
1988	Stefan Edberg
1989	Boris Becker
1990	Stefan Edberg
1991	Michael Stich
1992	**Andre Agassi** Andre Agassi started losing his hair at 19 and he wore hairpieces to hide it. The night before the 1990 French Open final, his wig was damaged. He wore it during the match but was so worried about it falling off that he lost.
1993-95	Pete Sampras
1996	Richard Krajicek
1997-'00	Pete Sampras
2001	**Goran Ivanišević** Ivanišević – unlucky? He once stood on a seashell; his foot became infected and needed surgery. Another time when retrieving his forgotten tennis racket, the door unexpectedly shut and broke several of his fingers.
2002	Lleyton Hewitt
2003-07	Roger Federer

Books of the Decade

Ten years that took you from kids' adventure books to dense works of profundity – or maybe just grown-up adventures! How many did you read when they were first published?

1972	**Watership Down by Richard Adams** Watership Down was the first story Adams ever wrote, at the age of 52, based on tales he told his daughters in the car.
1973	Gravity's Rainbow by Thomas Pynchon
1973	Crash: A Novel by J G Ballard
1974	**Tinker, Tailor, Soldier, Spy by John le Carré** David Cornwell, the man behind the pseudonym John le Carré, drew on his personal experience working for MI5 and MI6. He appeared as an extra in the film of the book.
1974	**Carrie by Stephen King** Carrie was King's first novel, published when he was 26. He disliked the first draft and threw it in the bin; his wife found it and encouraged him to continue with the story.
1974	The Bottle Factory Outing by Beryl Bainbridge
1975	Shogun by James Clavell
1975	The Periodic Table by Primo Levi
1976	Interview with the Vampire by Anne Rice
1977	Song of Solomon by Toni Morrison
1977	The Shining by Stephen King
1978	The World According to Garp by John Irving
1978	The Sea, The Sea by Iris Murdoch
1978	Tales of the City by Armistead Maupin
1979	**The Hitchhiker's Guide to the Galaxy by Douglas Adams** If 42 is the meaning of life, what's the meaning of 42? Nothing. Adams said it was simply a random number he chose. There's a message in there somewhere...
1979	A Bend in the River by V S Naipaul
1979	Sophie's Choice by William Styron
1980	A Confederacy of Dunces by John Kennedy Toole
1980	The Name of the Rose by Umberto Eco
1981	Midnight's Children by Salman Rushdie

Around the UK

Here's a round-up of the most newsworthy events from across the country in the year you turned (sweet) 16.

- ✦ Bulgarian dissident killed by poisoned brolly tip at Waterloo
- ✦ Ian Botham sets cricketing test-match record for runs and wickets
- ✦ Hitchhiker's Guide to the Galaxy debuts on Radio 4
- ✦ Sex Pistols break up after disastrous US tour
- ✦ Charity Motability set up to provide cars for disabled people
- ✦ Strikes temporarily close down BBC and Times newspaper
- ✦ Prince Andrew joins Royal Navy
- ✦ Police introduce new radar gun to catch speeding motorists (right)
- ✦ Ford car workers strike over pensions and pay
- ✦ Anna Ford becomes ITN's first female newsreader
- ✦ Naomi James becomes first woman to sail solo around world
- ✦ State Earnings-Related Pension scheme introduced
- ✦ Pacific island nation Tuvalu gains independence from UK
- ✦ Protected species status ends otter hunting
- ✦ Concrete cows erected in Milton Keynes
- ✦ Regular live broadcasts of parliament begin on BBC radio
- ✦ Louise Brown becomes world's first IVF 'test-tube' baby
- ✦ Bakers' strike leads to panic-buying of bread
- ✦ Viv Anderson first black footballer to play for England
- ✦ New Liverpool Cathedral completed
- ✦ Wave of strikes hits UK during Winter of Discontent
- ✦ US soldier 'walks' across English Channel in 'water' shoes

Born this year:
- ๕ Comic actor and TV host James Corden born in west London
- ๕ England and Aston Villa striker Emile Heskey born in Leicester
- ๕ Model and TV personality Katie Price born in Brighton

Lead poisoning has been known and observed for centuries but unleaded petrol didn't hit the forecourt until 1989 – and wasn't phased out globally until July 2021. This protester's particular cause was a lost one – the M25 was already opening in stages – but history is on her side.

With better roads come more opportunities to speed... until caught by new portable 'radar guns' which made their debut in 1978.

Stamps When You Were Young

Stamp collecting was the first serious hobby for many 20th century children. Commemorative issues weren't issued until the twenties, but soon became highly collectible – and the perfect gift for uncles in need of inspiration. These stamps may well have started your collection.

1924-5	**British Empire Exhibition** Designed to showcase Britain's strengths in an era of declining global influence, the exhibition left a legacy: the Empire Stadium (later renamed Wembley Stadium). The stamps were the UK's first commemorative issue, sixty years after the USA did the same.
1929	**9th Universal Postal Union Congress, London** Arguably of little interest to few outside philatelic circles, this was the first of several self-referential issues over successive decades. See also the Inter-Parliamentary stamps first issued in 1957.
1935	George V Silver Jubilee
1937	George VI Coronation
1940	**Centenary of the first adhesive postage stamp** Everyone has heard of the first adhesive stamp, issued in 1840: the Penny Black. (Perforations didn't come along until the 1854 Penny Red.) The glue on commemorative stamps contained around 14 calories!
1946	Victory
1948	Royal Silver Wedding
1948	Olympic Games
1949	The 75th Anniversary of the Universal Postal Union
1951	Festival of Britain
1951	George VI (high value 'definitives')
1953	The coronation of Queen Elizabeth II
1955	Castles (high value 'definitives')
1957	**World Scout Jamboree** Held in Sutton Coldfield; 50,000 Scouts attended. After heavy rain, the US Air Force was called in to help.
1957	46th Inter-Parliamentary Union Conference
1958	6th British Empire and Commonwealth Games

The Biggest Hits When You Were 16

The songs that topped the charts when you turned 16 might not be in your top 10 these days, but you'll probably remember them!

Uptown Top Ranking ♪ Althea and Donna
Figaro ♪ Brotherhood of Man
Take a Chance on Me ♪ ABBA
Wuthering Heights ♪ Kate Bush
Kate Bush was only 18 years old when she wrote her timeless track, Wuthering Heights.

Lowry's Song ♪ Brian and Michael
Night Fever ♪ Bee Gees
Night Fever and a slew of other disco classics by the Bee Gees would form the soundtrack of the John Travolta movie, Saturday Night Fever.

Rivers of Babylon ♪ Boney M
The lyrics to this disco classic are based on the Biblical Psalm 137:1-4 – which is about the Jewish people longing to return to their homeland.

Three Times a Lady ♪ Commodores
Dreadlock Holiday ♪ 10cc
Co-writer of the song Graham Gouldman has never been to a cricket match – despite proclaiming his love for the song in the first chorus of this 70s anthem.

Rat Trap ♪ The Boomtown Rats
Da Ya Think I'm Sexy? ♪ Rod Stewart
Mary's Boy Child ♪ Boney M

Gameshow Hosts of the Fifties and Sixties

Many of these men were semi-permanent fixtures, their voices and catchphrases almost as familiar as our family's. Some were full-time entertainers, born to the stage; others seemed rather less suited to the spotlight!

Ted Ray... ✖ (Joker's Wild)
and his son, Robin Ray ✖ (Face the Music)
Peter Wheeler ✖ (Crossword on Two, Call My Bluff)
Robert Robinson ✖ (Brain of Britain, Ask the Family)
McDonald Hobley ✖ (Come Dancing, It's a Knockout)
David Jacobs ✖ (Juke Box Jury)
Shaw Taylor ✖ (Password, Pencil and Paper)
Eamonn Andrews ✖ (Crackerjack!)
Roy Plomley ✖ (Many a Slip)
Gilbert Harding ✖ (Twenty Questions, What's My Line?)

Harding was a teacher and policeman before working in radio and television. Resentful of his fame, Harding was once left mortified on the London Underground when he was recognised by fellow passengers who failed to notice that TS Eliot was also in the same carriage.

Bamber Gascoigne ✖ (University Challenge)
Tommy Trinder ✖ (Sunday Night at the Palladium)
Bruce Forsyth ✖ (Beat the Clock)

Bruce Forsyth first appeared on television in 1939. He had many talents including playing the ukulele and accordion, singing, dancing and acting. In his later years, Forsyth stated that he regretted presenting so many gameshows.

Leslie Crowther ✖ (Billy Cotton Band Show, Crackerjack)
Bob Monkhouse ✖ (The Golden Shot)

While serving in the RAF, Bob Monkhouse drafted a letter to the BBC from his group captain, stating that 18-year-old Monkhouse was a war hero and deserved an audition. His group captain signed the letter without reading it; Monkhouse got his audition.

Hughie Green ✖ (Opportunity Knocks)
Derek Batey ✖ (Mr and Mrs)
Wilfred Pickles ✖ (radio show Have a Go)

Kitchen Inventions

The 20th-century kitchen was a playground for food scientists and engineers with new labour-saving devices and culinary shortcuts launched every year. Here are some our parents – and now you – wouldn't be without.

1929	**Dishwasher** The first hand-operated dishwasher was created in 1885 by inventor and socialite, Josephine Cochrane, who was tired of her servants chipping her fine china. In 1929, Miele brought out an electric, top-loading model. Front-loading and drying functions followed in 1940; automation in 1960.
1937	Blender
1939	Pressure cooker
1940	Chest freezer
1945	**Fridge** If you think today's American-style fridges are big, consider the Large Hadron Collider in Geneva. With a circumference of 17 miles and 9,300 magnets, it's chilled to -270C before use. That would definitely keep your milk cold.
1948	Kenwood mixer
1955	Automatic kettle
1956	**Non-stick pan** You can thank a French angler's wife for your non-stick pans: it was she who noticed her husband's habit of coating his gear in non-stick Teflon, and suggested he did the same to her pans. Scrambled egg fans owe her a life-long debt.
1960	**Tupperware** In 1960, Tupperware parties arrived in the UK. Earl Tupper's 1948 invention took off when a US single mother called Brownie Wise started home sales and the social selling concept proved equally successful here. This icon of female entrepreneurship was dismissed in 1958 for being too outspoken.
974	Microwave
974	Food processor
976	**Deep fat fryer** The Egyptians, Romans and Greeks were all known to have been keen on deep frying their food – often items that look uncommonly like today's doughnuts (minus the jam).

Around the World When You Turned 18

These are the headlines from around the globe as you were catapulted into adulthood.

- ✦ IRA inmates stage hunger strikes in Northern Ireland's prison
- ✦ War begins as Iraqi troops invade western Iran
- ✦ Robert Mugabe elected Zimbabwe prime minister
- ✦ 350 million watch TV soap Dallas to find out who shot JR
- ✦ Mount St Helens erupts in Washington State, USA
- ✦ Norwegian oil rig capsizes in North Sea, killing 123
- ✦ Australian baby Azaria Chamberlain missing in outback dingo case
- ✦ US leads Moscow Olympics boycott over USSR Afghanistan invasion
- ✦ General Tito's death triggers violent break-up of Yugoslavia
- ✦ Polish trade union Solidarity formed and shipyard workers strike
- ✦ Castro's Mariel Boatlift plan enables mass Cuban emigration to US
- ✦ Canary Island air crash kills all 146 UK holidaymakers on board
- ✦ World's first 24-hour TV news network CNN makes its debut
- ✦ Republican Ronald Reagan wins US presidency in landslide victory
- ✦ Indira Gandhi returns to power as prime minister of India
- ✦ Highest-earning arcade game Pac-Man released in Japan
- ✦ Fans head to Tbilisi for Russia's first official rock festival
- ✦ Tactile puzzle Rubik's Cube debuts at London toy fair

Born this year:
- ⚭ US tennis champion Venus Williams born in Lynwood, California
- ⚭ FC Barcelona's top scorer Lionel Messi born in Rosario, Argentina
- ⚭ Comedy actress Rebel Wilson born in Sydney, Australia
- ⚭ Canadian actor Ryan Gosling born in London, Ontario

Toys of Your Childhood

In the sixties, the toy industry got serious: no more lead paint. New licensing models (Thunderbirds! Batman! Doctor Who!). And a Toy of the Year award – the James Bond Aston Martin car was the first winner. Hop into the seventies and you'd soon be needing some batteries to go with some of those Christmas surprises…

Sindy
Katie Kopykat
Betta Bilda
Plasticraft
Peter Powell Stunter
Not to be confused with the popular Radio 1 DJ, Powell was a kite designer who hit the big time after one of his models was featured on the BBC show Nationwide. His revolutionary idea was to use two lines for added control. 'It tugs at the heart strings,' he told the BBC in 2014.

Playmobil
Action Man
Duplo
Spacehopper
Just sneaking into this decade (if Spacehoppers can sneak): these went on sale in 1969. Sold as Hoppity Hops in the USA. In 2018, Steven Payne crossed the Alps on one. Madness.

Ping Pong
Nerf ball
Skateboards
Lego
The world's biggest manufacturer of tyres is not Goodyear, or Michelin - it's Lego. They produce around 300 million tiny tyres every year.

Evel Knievel Stunt Cycle
Etch-a-Sketch
Magna Doodle
Simon
Speak and Spell
The Speak and Spell was the first mass-produced item to include a digital signal processor, a precursor to the computers we have in our homes today.

Around the UK

Voting. Placing a bet. Buying a legal drink. Turning 18 is serious stuff. Here's what everyone was reading about in the year you reached this milestone.

- ✦ UK unemployment tops two million
- ✦ SAS raid ends six-day Iranian Embassy hostage siege in London
- ✦ Brit Nigel Short, 14, becomes youngest international chess master
- ✦ Republican inmate Bobby Sands on hunger strike at Maze prison
- ✦ Reformist Robert Runcie appointed Archbishop of Canterbury
- ✦ Margaret Thatcher makes 'the lady's not for turning' speech
- ✦ Works closures signal end of Black Country steelmaking
- ✦ Second fire destroys much of London's Alexandra Palace
- ✦ Women's protest camp set up at Greenham Common missile base
- ✦ John Lennon shot dead in New York by obsessed fan (right)
- ✦ The Queen first UK monarch to make Vatican state visit
- ✦ Zimbabwe (Southern Rhodesia) gains independence from UK
- ✦ UK's biggest theme park Alton Towers opens
- ✦ Figure skater Robin Cousins wins gold at US Winter Olympics
- ✦ Celebrity bear Hercules goes missing on Scottish island
- ✦ Pirate radio ship Caroline runs aground in heavy seas
- ✦ First episode of BBC satirical sitcom Yes, Minister screened
- ✦ Steel workers stage first national strike in 50 years over pay
- ✦ Michael Foot takes over as Labour Party leader
- ✦ Inflation rises to 18%

Born this year:
- ⚭ Racing driver Jenson Button born in Frome, Somerset
- ⚭ Mezzo-soprano Katherine Jenkins born in Neath, Wales
- ⚭ Chancellor of Exchequer Rishi Sunak born in Southampton

Three days after John Lennon was shot and killed on December 8 1980, the shock is still written on the face of fans. They're gathered outside the Dakota Building in New York where Mark Chapman waited calmly to be arrested, holding a copy of The Catcher in the Rye. There was no funeral; in its place, Yoko requested ten minutes' silence. And on the following Sunday, every radio station in the city heeded her call.

Medical Advances Before You Were 21

A girl born in the UK in 1921 had a life expectancy of 59.6 years (boys: 55.6). By 2011 that was up to 82.8 (79 for boys), thanks to medical advances including many of these.

1962	Hip replacement, beta blockers
1963	**Valium**

Valium was famously dubbed 'mother's little helper' by The Rolling Stones. Valium was hailed as a wonder drug as it worked was a far less risky alternative to barbiturates.

1963	Lung transplant, artificial heart
1964	Measles vaccine
1965	**Portable defibrillator**

CPR on TV is successful one time in two, a 2009 study found: roughly the same as reality. However, the lack of follow-up or age-related differences on TV means people's expectation for a life-saving result is unrealistically high.

1966	Pancreas transplant
1967	Heart transplant
1968	Liver transplant, Controlled drug delivery
1969	**Cochlear implant**

Cochlear implants aren't always a success. Some can't get on with them; others believe they undermine deaf culture.

1969	Balloon catheter
1971	CAT scan
1972	Insulin pump
1973	MRI scanning, Laser eye surgery (LASIK)
1974	Depo-Provera contraceptive injection
1974	**Liposuction**

Liposuction did not take off until 1985 when techniques had improved to decrease the chance of serious bleeding.

1976	First commercial PET scanner
1978	Test-tube baby (IVF)
1980	MRI whole body scanner
1981	Heart-lung transplant
1982	Artificial heart

Popular Girls' Names

If you started a family at a young age, these are the names you're most likely to have chosen. And even if you didn't pick them, a lot of British parents did!

Sarah
Claire
Nicola
Emma
Lisa
Joanne
Michelle
Helen
Samantha

At number 9, Samantha's first appearance is among the highest of the century. She'll stay around until 2003.

Karen
Amanda
Rachel
Louise
Julie
Clare
Rebecca
Sharon
Victoria
Caroline
Susan
Alison
Catherine
Elizabeth
Deborah
Donna
Tracey
Tracy

Rising and falling stars:

Just like the boys, several names are all-too-briefly on the lips of many new parents: Vanessa, Nichola, Tara, Clair and Sonia.

Animals Extinct in Your Lifetime

Billions of passenger pigeons once flew the US skies.
By 1914, they had been trapped to extinction. Not every
species dies at our hands, but it's a sobering roll-call.
(Date is year last known alive or declared extinct).

1962	Red-bellied opossum, Argentina
1963	Kākāwahie honeycreeper, Hawaii
1964	South Island snipe, New Zealand
1966	Arabian ostrich
1967	Saint Helena earwig
1967	**Yellow blossom pearly mussel, USA** Habitat loss and pollution proved terminal for this resident of Tennessee.
1968	Mariana fruit bat (Guam)
1971	Lake Pedder earthworm, Tasmania
1972	Bushwren, New Zealand
1977	Siamese flat-barbelled catfish, Thailand
1979	Yunnan Lake newt, China
1981	Southern gastric-brooding frog, Australia
1986	Las Vegas dace
1989	Golden toad (see right)
1990	Atitlán grebe, Guatemala
1990	Dusky seaside sparrow, East Coast USA
1990s	Rotund rocksnail, USA
2000	**Pyrenean ibex, Iberia** For a few minutes in 2003 this species was brought back to life through cloning, but sadly the newborn female ibex died.
2001	Caspian tiger, Central Asia
2008	Saudi gazelle
2012	**Pinta giant tortoise** The rarest creature in the world for the latter half of his 100-year life, Lonesome George lived out his days in the Galapagos as the last remaining Pinta tortoise.
2016	Bramble Cay melomys (a Great Barrier Reef rodent)

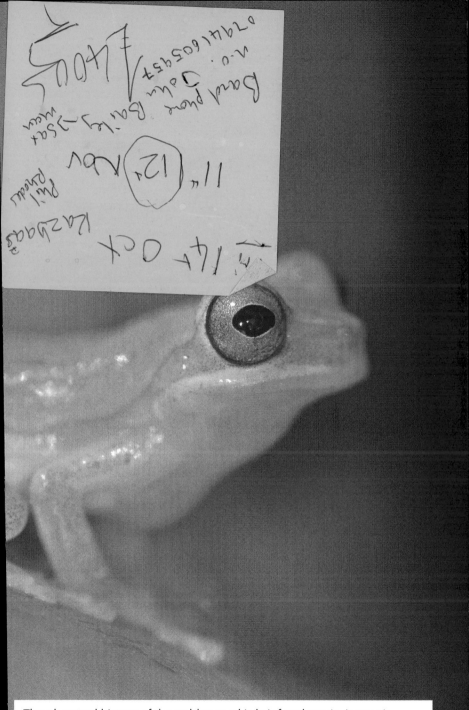

The observed history of the golden toad is brief and tragic. It wasn't discovered until 1964, abundant in a pristine area of Costa Rica. By 1989 it had gone, a victim of rising temperatures.

Popular Boys' Names

Here are the top boys' names for this year. In many instances it's merely a reshuffle of the popular names from the previous decade; but in the lower reaches, change is afoot…

Paul
After John, then David, came Paul: the nation's favourite name, but he'd keep the spot for less than a decade.

Mark
David
Andrew
Richard
Christopher
James
Simon
Michael
Matthew
Stephen
Lee
John
Robert
Darren
Daniel
Steven
Jason
Nicholas
Jonathan
Ian
Neil
Peter
Stuart
Anthony
Martin
Kevin

Rising and falling stars:
It's rare that names become popular enough to make the Top 100 only to fall out of favour as quickly as they came. Rarer still to have three flashes-in-the-pan: Glen, Brett and Damian.

Popular Movies When You Were 21

The biggest stars in the biggest movies: these are the films the nation was enjoying as you entered adulthood.

The Wicked Lady 🎞 Faye Dunaway, Alan Bates
Trading Places 🎞 Eddie Murphy, Dan Aykroyd
Ralph Bellamy and Don Ameche reprised their roles in Eddie Murphy's later movie, Coming to America. This time their characters appeared as two homeless people rather than millionaire investment brokers.

The Honorary Consul 🎞 Elpidia Carrillo, Richard Gere
Educating Rita 🎞 Julie Walters, Michael Caine
Cujo 🎞 Dee Wallace, Danny Pintauro
The titular St. Bernard was played by five different dogs, as well as a mechanical puppet and a stunt man in a dog costume.

Krull 🎞 Ken Marshall, Lysette Anthony
Tender Mercies 🎞 Robert Duvall, Tess Harper
WarGames 🎞 Matthew Broderick, Ally Sheedy
Flashdance 🎞 Jennifer Beals, Michael Nouri
The Outsiders 🎞 C Thomas Howell, Matt Dillon
Return of the Jedi 🎞 Mark Hamill, Harrison Ford
The word 'Ewok' is never spoken out loud in the movie.

The Champions 🎞 Yuen Biao, Moon Lee
The Dead Zone 🎞 Tom Skerritt, Christopher Walken
The Hunger 🎞 David Bowie, Catherine Deneuve
The Dresser 🎞 Edward Fox, Albert Finney
Risky Business 🎞 Tom Cruise, Rebecca De Mornay
Scarface 🎞 Al Pacino, Michelle Pfeiffer
The nickname 'Scarface' was a moniker for Al Capone, who serves as loose inspiration to the story.

Terms of Endearment 🎞 Shirley MacLaine, Debra Winger
Heat and Dust 🎞 Greta Scacchi, Julie Christie
Betrayal 🎞 Patricia Hodge, Jeremy Irons
Octopussy 🎞 Roger Moore, Maud Adams
The King of Comedy 🎞 Robert De Niro, Jerry Lewis
Never Say Never Again 🎞 Sean Connery, Kim Basinger

Around the UK

A selection of national headlines from the year you turned 21. But how many can you remember?

- ✦ BBC launches UK's first breakfast news programme Breakfast Time
- ✦ Scilly Isle helicopter crashes in thick fog, killing 20 onboard (right)
- ✦ UK heatwave brings consistently hot temperatures throughout July
- ✦ US cruise missiles arrive at Greenham Common amid protests
- ✦ Lester Piggott wins ninth Epsom Derby on Teenoso
- ✦ 38 IRA armed prisoners break out of Belfast's Maze Prison
- ✦ IRA car bomb explodes outside Harrods – killing six, injuring 90
- ✦ Seat belts compulsory for drivers and front-seat passengers
- ✦ Wheel clamps first used on UK streets
- ✦ Saharan dust creates blood-red rainstorms across UK
- ✦ Government expels three Russian spies
- ✦ Tory election landslide gives Thatcher second term in office
- ✦ Michael Foot resigns; Neil Kinnock becomes Labour Party leader
- ✦ £26m in gold stolen from Brinks-Mat vault at Heathrow
- ✦ £1 coin introduced in England and Wales
- ✦ First UK heart and lung transplant performed at Harefield Hospital
- ✦ First compact disks go on sale in UK shops
- ✦ Monster Raving Loony Party contests first seat in Bermondsey
- ✦ Trade Secretary Cecil Parkinson quits over lovechild scandal
- ✦ Serial killer Dennis Nilsen on trial after human remains found in drain
- ✦ Derby-winning stallion Shergar stolen

Born this year:
- ఴ Beehived singer-songwriter Amy Winehouse born in Enfield, London
- ఴ Devil Wears Prada actress Emily Blunt born in Roehampton, London
- ఴ Superman actor Henry Cavill born in St Helier, Jersey

The wreck of Sikorsky helicopter Oscar November is brought ashore at Falmouth after crashing into the sea off Scilly, killing 19 passengers and one crew member. Flying low under a blanket of fog without audible indicators of low altitude, the aircraft made an accidental descent and hit the water. The helicopter was fitted with sponsons - lateral projections to help it float if landing in water - but both sheared off, and the aircraft sank swiftly. Six adults and children managed to swim free. After an hour in the water, using suitcases as buoyancy aids, they were picked up by lifeboats.

The Biggest Hits When You Were 21

The artists you love at 21 are with you for life. How many of these hits from this milestone year can you still hum or sing in the bath?

You Can't Hurry Love 🎤 Phil Collins
Down Under 🎤 Men at Work
In 2010, Men at Work were forced to hand over 5% of royalties dating back to 2002. The successful claimant was the copyright owner of a traditional song Kookaburra that included the distinctive flute solo; they were alerted by press enquiries after a TV quiz question revealed the embedded riff.

Too Shy 🎤 Kajagoogoo
Billie Jean 🎤 Michael Jackson
Michael Jackson performed his first ever televised moonwalk during a performance of Billie Jean in 1983.

Total Eclipse of the Heart 🎤 Bonnie Tyler
Let's Dance 🎤 David Bowie
Let's Dance was produced by disco legend and Chic guitarist, Nile Rodgers.

Every Breath You Take 🎤 The Police
Baby Jane 🎤 Rod Stewart
Wherever I Lay My Hat 🎤 Paul Young
Give It Up 🎤 KC and the Sunshine Band
Karma Chameleon 🎤 Culture Club
Uptown Girl 🎤 Billy Joel
The uptown girls in question were his girlfriend at the time – Elle Macpherson – and his wife-to-be, Christie Brinkley, who appeared in the video, set in a car repair workshop.

Only You 🎤 The Flying Pickets

Popular Food in the 1960s

Convenient ready meals, 'fancy foreign food'... the sixties menu had it all. The chemists joined the dinner party, too, with additives and processes that made our new favourites easy and cheap to produce. We'd take a while to work out if this was always such a good idea!

Vesta curry or Chow Mein

Lager
'Lager' comes from the German word 'lagern', meaning 'to store', as lager takes longer to produce than other ales.

Coco Pops

Fish fingers
The largest fish finger ever made was 6ft long and weighed 136 kg. No word on whether the chef dipped it in ketchup.

Spaghetti Bolognese
You shouldn't include oregano, basil or garlic in the 'ragu' (not bolognese). And for goodness' sake, use tagliatelle, not spaghetti. Or... accept that it is as inauthentic as the Vesta curry and enjoy, like millions of Brits learned to do in the sixties.

Chicken Tikka Masala

Cheese and onion crisps
The first flavoured crisps were created by Joe 'Spud' Murphy (founder of Irish brand Taytos) in the late 1950s.

Crêpe Suzette

Chicken liver pâté

Angel Delight
Angel Delight doubled the dessert market when it was invented in 1967. Wallace and Gromit gave it another push in 1999.

Fray Bentos pies

Instant coffee

Frozen vegetables
Clarence Birdseye was the first person to freeze food for mass production, having got the idea from an Inuit in 1912.

Swedish meatballs

White bread
A new Chorleywood process introduced enzymes and additives and high-speed mixing. The result? Soft, cheap bread that sticks to the roof of your mouth. A nation couldn't get enough of it.

Fashion in the Sixties

As a child, you (generally) wear what you're given. It's only in hindsight, on fading slides, that you recognize that your outfits carried the fashion imprint of the day. Whether you were old or bold enough to carry off a pair of bell bottoms, though, is a secret that between you and your photo albums!

Shift dresses
Mini skirt
Popularised by Mary Quant who named the skirt after her favourite car - although not everyone was a fan. Coco Chanel described the skirt as 'just awful', and it was banned in some European countries.

Five-point cut
Vidal Sassoon
Sassoon had a temper. He would give clients a slap of a comb if they touched their hair while he was cutting it.

John Bates
Biba
Biba started as a mail order business, advertising a pink gingham dress in the Daily Mirror. 17,000 orders were placed and a shop was opened. On its opening day, the store sold out of its only product line.

St Michael American Tan tights
Dr Scholl
Orlon, Crimplene, Terylene, Spandex, PVC and Vinyl
Paper dresses
Twiggy
Jackie Kennedy
In 1962, Jackie Kennedy wore a leopard print coat which caused a spike in demand for leopard skin, leading to the death of up to 250,000 leopards. The coat's designer, Oleg Cassini, felt guilty about it for the rest of his life.

Little black dress
First introduced by Coco Chanel in the 1920s, the little black dress received a fifties update from Christian Dior. Audrey Hepburn's LBD sold for £467,200 in 2006.

Jean Shrimpton
Jane Birkin

Around the World When You Turned 25

By your mid-twenties, TV coverage of news in far-flung places brought global stories into our homes almost as fast as they happened. How many do you remember?

- Ferry Herald of Free Enterprise capsizes off Zeebrugge – 193 die
- AIDS drug AZT approved for use in USA
- Cartoon family The Simpsons make US debut on Tracey Ullman Show
- Terrorist bus station bomb kills over 100 in Colombo, Sri Lanka
- American Lynne Cox first to swim Bering Strait from US to USSR
- Work on UK-France's Channel Tunnel begins
- US toddler rescued after 58 hours trapped in well
- Black Monday sees stock markets around world crash
- First Rugby World Cup co-hosted by Australia and New Zealand
- 400 killed as Shia pilgrims and Saudi police clash during Hajj
- French court gives Nazi war criminal Klaus Barbie life sentence
- Anti-depressant drug Prozac approved for use in USA
- Filipino ferry Doña Paz crashes into oil tanker – over 4,000 dead
- UK peace envoy Terry Waite held by Islamic militia in Beirut
- German teen flies into Soviet airspace to land in Red Square
- Israeli occupation of West Bank and Gaza triggers first intifada
- Vietnam war film Platoon wins Best Picture Oscar

Born this year:
- Atlético Madrid striker Luis Suárez born in Salto, Uruguay
- Champion tennis player Novak Djokovic born in Belgrade, Serbia
- US actor Zac Efron born San Luis Obispo, California

Cars of your Childhood (Pt.2)

Whether you were in one or just pointing from the side of the road, cars of the sixties truly delivered; for every trusted Hillman Imp or Vauxhall Victor, the decade boasts a glamorous Aston Martin DB5 or a covetable Jaguar E-type.

Mini
Famously featured in the 1969 film The Italian Job, Mini manufacturer BMC didn't want the car used in the film and refused to donate any. However, the director insisted that British cars should be used in a British film and over a dozen were used.

Triumph Herald

Vauxhall Victor
The design of the Vauxhall Victor was based on the style of American cars, which didn't appeal to everyone's taste in 1960s Britain. The car also gained a negative reputation for rusting.

Austin 1100

Sunbeam Tiger

Aston Martin DB5
The Aston Martin DB5 has been described as the most famous car in the world, following its 1964 debut in Goldfinger. In 1968, the car used by James Bond in the film was stripped of the weapons and gadgets and resold as a used car. It was stolen in 1997 and is rumoured to be in the Middle East.

Hillman Hunter

Lotus Elan
The Lotus Elan was designed by Ron Hickman, who subsequently left Lotus and went on to design the Black & Decker Workmate. Early versions of the Elan were also available as a kit that could be assembled by the buyer.

Ford Cortina
The Ford Cortina was launched in 1962 and later proved to be the best-selling car of the 1970s in its Mk3 guise. Designed as a new version of the Ford Consul, the name was changed to Cortina after the Italian ski resort Cortina d'Ampezzo, host to the 1956 Winter Olympics.

Rover 3500

MGB

Vauxhall HA Viva

Books of the Decade

Were you a voracious bookworm in your twenties? Or a more reluctant reader, only drawn by the biggest titles of the day? Here are the new titles that fought for your attention.

1982	The Color Purple by Alice Walker
1982	**Schindler's Ark by Thomas Keneally**

Keneally wrote Schindler's Ark - later retitled Schindler's List - after he met Holocaust survivor Leopold Page. Schindler is credited with saving over 1,000 lives.

1983	The Colour of Magic by Terry Pratchett
1983	Waterland by Graham Swift
1984	Money by Martin Amis
1984	Neuromancer by William Gibson
1984	The Wasp Factory by Iain Banks
1985	**The Handmaid's Tale by Margaret Atwood**

The Communist reign of Nicolae Ceaușescu in Romania partially inspired Atwood to write The Handmaid's Tale. While he was in power, women had to have four babies; abortions were illegal, contraception was banned, and women were examined for signs of pregnancy at work.

1985	Blood Meridian by Cormac McCarthy
1985	Perfume by Patrick Suskind
1986	The Old Devils by Kingsley Amis
1986	It by Stephen King
1987	Beloved by Toni Morrison
1987	Bonfire of the Vanities by Tom Wolfe
1988	Satanic Verses by Salman Rushdie
1988	The Alchemist by Paulo Coelho
1988	Oscar and Lucinda by Peter Carey
1988	The Swimming-Pool Library by Alan Hollinghurst
1989	A Prayer for Owen Meany by John Irving
1989	The Remains of the Day by Kazuo Ishiguro
1989	London Fields by Martin Amis
1990	Possession by AS Byatt
1990	The Buddha of Suburbia by Hanif Kureishi
1991	Regeneration by Pat Barker
1991	American Psycho by Bret Easton Ellis

Stamps in the Sixties

The UK hit its stride with commemorative stamps in the sixties. There were dry centenary and congress issues, but in 1965 the Postmaster General, Tony Benn, removed the need to include a large monarch portrait. The result? The kind of stamps every young collector would want.

1963	Freedom From Hunger
1963	Lifeboat Conference
1963	Red Cross Centenary Congress
1964	Opening of the Forth Road Bridge
1965	Winston Churchill Commemoration
1965	700th anniversary of Parliament
1965	Centenary of the Salvation Army
1965	**Antiseptic Surgery Centenary** Celebrates the introduction of surgical sterilisation by Joseph Lister.
1965	Commonwealth Arts Festival
1965	25th Anniversary of the Battle of Britain
1965	Opening of the Post Office Tower
1966	Westminster Abbey
1966	Landscapes
1966	**1966 World Cup** Stamps to mark England's role as hosts were hastily reissued in August 1966 with ENGLAND WINNERS added
1966	British birds
1966	British technology
1966	900th anniversary of the Battle of Hastings
1966	**Christmas** The first UK Christmas stamps. The idea was championed by Tony Benn and the stamps designed by two 6-year-old – winners of a Blue Peter competition.
1967	British wild flowers
1967	British paintings
1967	British discoveries and inventions
1967	Sir Francis Chichester's solo circumnavigation
1968	British bridges
1969	Concorde's first flight

Sixties TV Gameshows

Gameshows in the sixties were dominated by a few stalwarts, though a few short-lived experimental formats and US adaptions were tried. Without any serious competition, audiences were enormous. How many do you remember watching with your family?

Call My Bluff
Almost every episode from the first eight series of Call My Bluff has been wiped from the BBC archives. There were 263 episodes in series one to eight, and only seven episodes still survive.

Face the Music

Just a Minute

Ask the Family

University Challenge
Several celebrities appeared on University Challenge before they became famous. These include Stephen Fry, David Starkey, Sebastian Faulks, Julian Fellowes, and Miriam Margolyes (who swore when she answered a question incorrectly). University Challenge has a claim to be the longest running TV quiz show, alongside A Question of Sport.

For Love or Money

Mr and Mrs
After watching the Canadian version of Mr and Mrs, Derek Batey was inspired to develop a UK version of the show for Border Television. Batey hosted over 500 episodes, as well as 5,000 on stage after developing a theatrical version.

Play Your Hunch

Take Your Pick

Brain of Britain

Double Your Money
A November 1966 episode drew the nation's highest gameshow audience of nearly 20 million viewers.

Exit! It's the Way-Out Show

Many a Slip

Three Little Words

Crossword on 2

Around the UK

25

Mid twenties: that's adulthood by anybody's reckoning. Were you reading the news, or making it? Here are the national stories that dominated the front pages.

+ Peace envoy Terry Waite taken hostage in Lebanon
+ Gunman Michael Ryan kills 14 in Hungerford, Berkshire
+ Margaret Thatcher secures third term as prime minister
+ Police clamp down on illegal Acid House raves
+ London's driverless Dockland Light Railway opens
+ Rick Astley's Never Gonna Give You Up tops UK charts
+ Hurricane-force winds batter southern England
+ IRA Remembrance Day bomb kills 11 in Enniskillen
+ Escalator fire at London's King's Cross Station kills 31 (right)
+ Government phases out coal-mine canaries
+ London City Airport opens in Docklands
+ Christie's London sells Van Gogh Sunflowers for £25m
+ Ford takes over luxury sports car firm Aston Martin
+ Jockey Lester Piggott jailed for tax evasion
+ Scandi furniture firm IKEA opens first store in Warrington
+ 'Party planner' Cynthia Payne not guilty of 'brothel' charges
+ £1m Operation Deepscan fails to find Loch Ness Monster
+ 20 million tune in as Hilda Ogden leaves Coronation Street

Born this year:
- England and Leicester City striker Jamie Vardy born in Sheffield
- Soul singer Joss Stone born in Dover, Kent
- Tennis champion Andy Murray born in Glasgow
- Singer Emeli Sandé born in Sunderland, England

Cross by Public Subway

to

NORTHERN, PICCADILLY
VICTORIA, METROPOLITAN
& CIRCLE LINES

LONDON TRANSPORT TRAVEL ENQUIRIES

and Public Lavatories

A dropped cigarette falls into grease and litter beneath a wooden escalator. A fire on some scale was inevitable. But the speed and ferocity of the blaze at Kings Cross Underground station was literally unimaginable; it spread through a previously unknown spouting phenomenon that drives fire up an incline, called the trench effect. A fireball burst from the staircase into the ticket hall, still crowded with evening commuters. Thirty-one people died.

The Biggest Hits When You Were 30

How many of these big tunes from the year you turned thirty will still strike a chord decades later?

Goodnight Girl 🎤 Wet Wet Wet

Stay 🎤 Shakespears Sister

Deeply Dippy 🎤 Right Said Fred

Deeply Dippy was the only Right Said Fred song to top the charts in the UK – their better-known song I'm Too Sexy only reached number two.

Please Don't Go 🎤 KWS

Abba-esque 🎤 Erasure

Ain't No Doubt 🎤 Jimmy Nail

Rhythm Is a Dancer 🎤 Snap!

Ebeneezer Goode 🎤 The Shamen

This controversial song about the pleasures and perils of the drug Ecstasy was eventually withdrawn, ending its reign at number one.

Sleeping Satellite 🎤 Tasmin Archer

End of the Road 🎤 Boyz II Men

Would I Lie to You? 🎤 Charles and Eddie

Would I Lie to You went to number one in 16 countries.

I Will Always Love You 🎤 Whitney Houston

Whitney Houston covered this Dolly Parton classic for the 1992 movie, The Bodyguard, which she also starred in. It became the best-selling single of all time for any female artist.

...and the Movies You Saw That Year, Too

From award winners to crowd pleasers, here are the movies that played as your third decade drew to a close.

Glengarry Glen Ross 🎟 Jack Lemmon, Al Pacino
Alec Baldwin's famously venomous monologue lasts over seven minutes.

Batman Returns 🎟 Michael Keaton, Danny DeVito
Barton Fink 🎟 John Turturro, John Goodman
The Coen brothers wrote this script in three weeks while suffering from writer's block on Miller's Crossing.

Bill & Ted's Bogus Journey 🎟 Keanu Reeves, Alex Winter
The Muppet Christmas Carol 🎟 Michael Caine, Frank Oz
Patriot Games 🎟 Harrison Ford, Sean Bean
JFK 🎟 Kevin Costner, Gary Oldman
Cape Fear 🎟 Robert De Niro, Nick Nolte
Unforgiven 🎟 Clint Eastwood, Gene Hackman
Eastwood postponed this film for years because he wanted to be old enough to play the lead role himself.

Wayne's World 🎟 Mike Myers, Dana Carvey
Howards End 🎟 Anthony Hopkins, Emma Thompson
Of Mice and Men 🎟 Gary Sinise, John Malkovich
White Men Can't Jump 🎟 Wesley Snipes, Woody Harrelson
Chaplin 🎟 Robert Downey Jr., Geraldine Chaplin
Basic Instinct 🎟 Michael Douglas, Sharon Stone
The Crying Game 🎟 Stephen Rea, Jaye Davidson
The Hand That Rocks the Cradle
The Last of the Mohicans 🎟 Daniel Day-Lewis, Madeleine Stowe
Day-Lewis learned how to skin animals, throw tomahawks and build canoes for his role in this movie.

Frankie and Johnny 🎟 Al Pacino, Michelle Pfeiffer
The Bodyguard 🎟 Kevin Costner, Whitney Houston
Death Becomes Her 🎟 Meryl Streep, Bruce Willis
Home Alone 2: Lost in New York 🎟 Macaulay Culkin, Joe Pesci
Single White Female 🎟 Bridget Fonda, Jennifer Jason Leigh
1492: Conquest of Paradise 🎟 Gérard Depardieu, Armand Assante

Around the House

Sometimes with a fanfare but often by stealth, inventions and innovations transformed the 20th-century household. Here's what arrived between the ages of 10 and 30.

1972	Scientific calculators
1973	BIC lighter
1974	Sticky notes
1975	Betamax movies
1976	**VHS movies** The last film ever released on VHS was David Cronenberg's 2006 thriller, A History of Violence.
1977	Sony Walkman
1977	Auto focus cameras
1978	Electronic (computer-controlled) sewing machines
1978	Slide Away (sofa) beds
1979	**Black + Decker DustBuster** Black + Decker came up with the idea of a cordless vacuum while working on a cordless drill for NASA.
1979	Shake n' Vac
1982	CD Players
1983	Dyson bagless vacuum cleaner
1983	**Nintendo Entertainment System (NES)** Super Mario Bros is the best-selling NES game of all time.
1984	Sony Discman (changed to CD Walkman in 1999)
1985	Shower radio
1988	Sega Megadrive
1989	Game Boy
1990	Self-wringing mop The 2015 film Joy was based on Joy Mangano, the creator of the self-wringing mop – the Miracle Mop.
1991	Memory foam mattresses
1992	ThighMaster This nineties fad was invented by the heir to the Reynolds Tobacco company. Six million were sold through celebrity endorsement.

British Prime Ministers in Your Lifetime

These are the occupants of 10 Downing Street, London, during your lifetime, not including Larry the resident cat. Don't be deceived by that unassuming, black, blast-proof door: Number 10 features a warren of more than 100 rooms.

1957–63	**Harold Macmillan** Macmillan was the scion of a wealthy publishing family, but the biggest secret of his life was kept under wraps: his wife Dorothy's 30-year affair with fellow Conservative (and Krays associate) Robert Boothby. Macmillan died aged 92; his last words were, 'I think I will go to sleep now.'
1963–64	Sir Alec Douglas-Home
1964–70	Harold Wilson
1970–74	Edward Heath
1974–76	Harold Wilson
1976–79	James Callaghan
1979–90	**Margaret Thatcher** 'Today we were unlucky,' said the chilling statement from the IRA, 'but remember we only have to be lucky once.' The 1994 bombing of the Grand hotel in Brighton may not have killed the prime minister, but five others died and others were left with lifelong injuries.
1990–97	John Major
1997–2007	Tony Blair
2007–10	**Gordon Brown** Brown has no sight in his left eye after being kicked in a school rugby game; in 2009, while prime minister, rips in the right retina were also diagnosed.
2010–16	David Cameron
2016–19	**Theresa May** Asked in a pre-election interview about the naughtiest thing she'd ever done, May said that she'd once run through a field of wheat with her friends, and that the farmers 'weren't too happy'.
2019–	Boris Johnson

Household Goods in 1962

In 1947, the government calculated inflation for the first time using a basket of frequently purchased goods. This lis has been reviewed ever since; the changes mirror our ever changing tastes and habits. Here's what housewives were buying when you were small.

Sliced white bread
Chocolate coated biscuits
Dry cleaning
Potato crisps
Crisps entered the basket of goods in 1962, the same year Golden Wonder (bought by Imperial Tobacco) launched cheese and onion flavoured crisps. Golden Wonder, Smith's and soon Walkers fought for the market, and consumption rocketed.

Oven ready chicken
Cuts of halibut
Second-hand car
Welfare milk scheme
Ground coffee
Frozen croquettes
As more homes had freezers and the desire for ready meals increased, frozen food was all the rage. Frozen croquettes were released in the early 1960s and were a resounding success.

Canned fruit salad
Canned fruit salad was designed to use the fruit scraps that couldn't be used in canning. Fruit salad arrived in the 1940s and became one of the most popular canned fruits available. You could even use it to make a fruit salad cake.

TV set rental
Gloss paint
Ceiling paper
Jeans
Latex backed carpet
Refrigerator
Ready-made suit
Terylene slacks
Created in Manchester in 1941, Terylene revolutionised clothing in the 1950s. It was used by Mary Quant to make the original miniskirts, and Ray Davies of The Kinks advertised it.

Popular Food in the 1970s

Jump into the next decade and it's time to roll out the hostess trolley. If it's not highly processed, artificially coloured, moulded and served in a novelty dish, is it even food? Still, most of it went down very well with the kids – and still does today, given half a chance.

Lemon meringue pie

Cheese and pineapple

Black Forest Gâteau

The Black Forest Gâteau is named after the kirsch alcohol made from Black Forest sour cherries, rather than the Black Forest region in Germany.

Dream Topping

Mateus Rose, Liebfraumilch and Chianti

Cornetto

Cornetto cones were created by Spica, an Italian ice-cream company, in 1976. The company was bought by Unilever not long after, who then marketed the dessert in Europe.

Quavers

Quiche

Unlike the gâteau above, quiche Lorraine *was* named after the area in which it was created. It is considered a French dish, even though Lorraine was under German rule at the time.

Pot Noodle

The original Pot Noodle made in 1979 did not contain a sauce sachet - these were only added in 1992.

Fondue

Smash

Scampi in a basket

Banoffee pie

Chili con carne

Chili is the state dish of Texas, where many people think the recipe originated. Before WWII, hundreds of individual parlours all insisted they had their own secret recipe.

Prawn cocktails

Profiteroles

The Full English Breakfast

Beer of the Seventies

You could haul a seven-pint tin of Watneys Party Seven to a celebration. Someone would be drinking bland Watneys Red, or Courage Tavern ('It's what your right arm's for'). But how about a drop of that cold, refreshing lager you tried on holiday? 'Mine's a pint!' said millions of Brits.

Watneys Party Seven
Whitbread Tankard
Watneys Red
Double Diamond

Carlsberg
The inventor of Carlsberg, JC Jacobsen, gave a Ted Talk on his life philosophy in 2017 – 130 years after he died. He was brought back to life via hologram and even fielded questions from the audience.

Heineken
The Heineken International company owns more than 250 other brands, many of which you'll probably recognise such as Amstel, Desperados and Strongbow.

Tennant's Gold Label

Guinness
When Arthur Guinness started his now-famous business he rented an unused brewery on a 9,000-year lease – though the contract was eventually voided when the company bought the land and surrounding areas to expand the business.

Worthington E
Carling Black Label
Harp
Stella Artois
Ind Coope Super
Younger's Scotch Ale
Bass Charrington

Strongbow
HP Bulmer named his drink after one of the greatest knights in English history, Richard de Clare, who was given the nickname Strongbow.

Long Life

Seventies TV Gameshows

With light entertainment increasingly becoming the bedrock of TV channel success, the seventies saw an explosion of formats from gimmicks to US imports. Which ones got you shouting at the telly?

It's a Knockout
Although this show began in 1966 and it limped on into the new century, the seventies was It's a Knockout's golden age, thanks in no small part to presenter Stuart Hall. The winning teams proceeded to represent the UK at the European final, Jeux Sans Frontières.

I'm Sorry I Haven't a Clue
Jokers Wild
My Music

A Question of Sport
A Question of Sport is the world's longest running TV sports quiz. The first episode was recorded in 1970 in a converted chapel in Rusholme, Manchester, and the show is still recorded in the city as it surpasses 1,300 episodes.

Quote... Unquote
Whodunnit?
Mastermind
Screen Test

Celebrity Squares
Inspired by the game noughts and crosses, Celebrity Squares was based on the US gameshow Hollywood Squares. The original run was presented by Bob Monkhouse, who also returned to host the revival of the show in the 1990s.

Gambit
The Generation Game
The Golden Shot
The Indoor League
Password
Runaround
Sale of the Century
The Sky's the Limit
Winner Takes All

Popular Boys' Names

Just as middle age crept up unnoticed, so the most popular names also evolved. The traditional choices – possibly including yours – were fast losing their appeal to new parents.

Jack
This is Jack's seventh year on top. He'll remain the nation's first choice from 1996 to 2008.

Joshua
Thomas
James
Daniel
Benjamin
Samuel
Joseph
William
Oliver
Harry
Matthew
Luke
Lewis
George
Callum
Adam
Ethan
Alexander
Ryan
Ben
Mohammed
Liam
Nathan
Jake
Connor

Rising and falling stars:
While names fell in and out of fashion in great numbers in the eighties and nineties, the pace has slowed. New this year: Finlay (and Finley), Leo, Sebastian and Gabriel. Out: Jason, Ashley and Peter.

Popular Girls' Names

It's a similar story for girls' names. Increasing numbers took their infant inspiration from popular culture. The worlds of music, film and now the internet are all fertile hunting grounds for those in need of inspiration.

Chloe
This is the last of six years on top for Chloe.

Emily
Jessica
Ellie
Sophie
Megan
Charlotte
Hannah
Olivia
Lucy
Lauren
Holly
Katie
Amy
Molly
Ella
Bethany
Rebecca
Grace
Mia
Georgia
Abigail
Caitlin
Leah
Amelia
Eleanor
Emma
Lily

Rising and falling stars:
Aaliyah, Lara and Zara: welcome to the Top 100!
Danielle, Gabrielle, Ellen, Natalie and Stephanie: we're afraid your time is up.

F1 Champions

If you fancy your chances in Formula One, start young. Sebastian Vettel won at 23. *El Maestro*, Juan Manuel Fangio, is the oldest winner to date, at 46. The field is wide open for an older champ, right?

Alain Prost 🏆 (1985-6,89,93)
Nelson Piquet 🏆 (1981,83,87)
Nelson Piquet lost his civilian driving licence in 2007 due to numerous speeding and parking offences. He was ordered to attend a week of lessons and pass an exam.

Ayrton Senna 🏆 (1988,90-1)
Two days before Senna's fatal crash at Imola, he was early to the scene of a near-fatal crash for Rubens Barrichello. One day before, he inspected the car of Roland Ratzenberger as the mortally-injured Austrian was taken to hospital – the same facility that would attempt to save Senna's life the following day after his crash on the same corner. An Austrian flag was later found in Senna's cockpit, intended to be unfurled as a tribute to Ratzenberger.

Nigel Mansell 🏆 (1992)
Michael Schumacher 🏆 (1994-5,2000-04)
Michael Schumacher was one of a handful of drivers to appear as themselves in the Pixar film Cars, voicing a Ferrari F430.

Damon Hill 🏆 (1996)
Jacques Villeneuve 🏆 (1997)
Mika Häkkinen 🏆 (1998-99)
Fernando Alonso 🏆 (2005-6)
A Fernando Alonso Sports Complex in Spain includes a museum dedicated to Alonso, a karting circuit, and a golf course.

Kimi Räikkönen 🏆 (2007)
Lewis Hamilton 🏆 (2008,14-15,17-20)

Fashion in the Seventies

he decade that taste forgot? Or a kickback against the
xties and an explosion of individuality? Skirts got shorter
nd longer). Block colours and peasant chic vied with
equins and disco glamour. How many of your seventies
utfits would you still wear today?

Flares
Platform shoes
Laura Ashley
While working as a secretary, Laura Ashley was inspired to
produce printed fabric after seeing a display at the Victoria and
Albert Museum. Struggling to make a profit, Laura Ashley and
her husband and children once lived in tents in Wales for
six months.

Gucci
Diane Von Furstenberg
Tie Dye
Kaftans
Brought to western culture via the hippie trail, the kaftan's
popularity was boosted further when Elizabeth Taylor wore a
kaftan-inspired dress for her second wedding to Richard Burton
in 1975.

Liza Minnelli
Lurex and suede
David Bowie
Afro, braids or a perm
Jumpsuit
Sequin hot pants
Moon boots
Double denim
Double denim garnered the nickname the 'Canadian tuxedo'
after Bing Crosby was refused entry to a hotel in Vancouver
because he wore a denim ensemble. Levi subsequently
designed Crosby a denim tuxedo.

Vivienne Westwood
Previously a primary school teacher, Vivienne Westwood lived
in an ex-council flat in Clapham until 2000. Her son from her
relationship with Malcolm McLaren founded lingerie brand
Agent Provocateur.

Household Goods in 1970

Frozen foods and eating out swallow up an increasingly larger share of the family budget in the seventies. Or how about a day trip (don't forget your AA membership and your mac), then home for a sweet sherry?

Frozen chicken

Mushrooms

Frozen beans

Sherry

Sherry consumption peaked in the UK in the 1970s following the development of sweet versions – often using added syrups or sugars – known as creams and developed for British palates.

Night storage heater

Plastic Mackintosh

MOT test

Introduced in 1960, the MOT was designed to test the brakes, lights, and steering of all vehicles over 10 years old. This was progressively reduced to every three years by 1967, and the test changed to include tyres.

State school meal

Canteen meal

Cup of tea

The 1970s saw a significant increase in eating out, so a cup of tea was added to the basket. Despite Britain's reputation as tea lovers, coffee sales overtook tea sales for the first time in 1986.

Cafe sandwich

Local authority rent

Local authority rent was added to the basket of goods in the 1970s; by 1979, 42% of Britons lived in council homes.

Paper handkerchiefs

Auto association subs

Keg of ale

Fresh cream

Gammon

While gammon gained popularity during the 1970s due to its unlikely pairing with pineapple rings, the word 'gammon' is now also used as an insult towards the political right, coined in response to 'snowflake'.

Post-war Chocolate

You'll find nearly all of these on the supermarket shelves, even though the most recently invented chocolate bar here was brought to market thirty years ago. Gulp.

1948	Fudge
1951	**Bounty**

If you wanted to sell a chocolate bar with curved ends and swirls on the top, in theory there's nothing that maker Mars could do to stop you: the shape was decreed not distinctive enough to trademark in 2009. Do check with a lawyer first, though.

1957	Munchies
1958	Picnic
1962	**After Eight Mint Chocolate Thins**

A billion of these are churned out every year (although we've never heard anyone call them chocolate thins).

1962	Topic
1963	Toffee Crisp
1967	Twix
1970	Chomp
1970	Curly Wurly
1973	Freddo
1976	**Double Decker**

Double Deckers contain raisins, don't they? Not any more: they were removed from the recipe during the eighties.

1976	Starbar
1976	**Yorkie**

'It's not for girls,' said the adverts. The sexist marketing of Yorkie reached its peak - or trough - in 2005 with special pink editions. By 2011 the complaints outweighed the commercial advantage. The 'men only' angle was dropped.

1978	Lion Bar
1980	Drifter
1983	**Wispa**

For twenty years, Wispa was the go-to Aero alternative. But then in 2003 it was gone. A predictable outcry followed and in 2007 it was back on the shelves. Phew.

1992	Time Out

Books of the Decade

Family, friends, TV, and more: there are as many midlife distractions as there are books on the shelf. Did you get drawn in by these bestsellers, all published in your thirties?

1992	The Secret History by Donna Tartt
1992	All the Pretty Horses by Cormac McCarthy
1992	The English Patient by Michael Ondaatje
1993	The Shipping News by E Annie Proulx
1993	Birdsong by Sebastian Faulks
1993	Paddy Clarke Ha Ha Ha by Roddy Doyle
1994	A Suitable Boy by Vikram Seth
1994	Snow Falling on Cedars by David Guterson
1995	A Fine Balance by Rohinton Mistry
1996	Infinite Jest by David Foster Wallace
1996	**A Game of Thrones by George RR Martin** The idea for the story came to Martin as a child through his pet turtles. They lived in a toy castle, and he pretended they were kings, lords and knights.
1996	Bridget Jones's Diary by Helen Fielding
1997	**Harry Potter And The Philosopher's Stone by J K Rowling** In the film of the book, Rik Mayall played the part of Peeves the Poltergeist. The scene was cut before release.
1997	American Pastoral by Philip Roth
1997	The God of Small Things by Arundhati Roy
1997	Underworld by Don DeLillo
1997	Memoirs of a Geisha by Arthur Golden
1997	Blindness by José Saramago
1998	The Poisonwood Bible by Barbara Kingsolver
1999	Disgrace by J M Coetzee
1999	Being Dead by Jim Crace
1999	Ghostwritten by David Mitchell
2000	White Teeth by Zadie Smith
2000	The Blind Assassin by Margaret Atwood
2001	Atonement by Ian McEwan
2001	The Corrections by Jonathan Franzen
2001	Austerlitz by W G Sebald

TV Newsreaders: The Early Days

Trusted, familiar, and mostly with received pronunciation: these are the faces that brought you and your family the news, and the dates they shuffled their papers.

Richard Baker 📺 (1954-82)
In 1954, Baker introduced the BBC's first TV news broadcast. Seventies children know his voice as the narrator of Mary, Mungo and Midge.

Robert Dougall 📺 (1955-73)
Kenneth Kendall 📺 (1955-69)
Angela Rippon 📺 (1975-2002)
The UK's first regular female newsreader and known nationwide for her 1976 Morecambe and Wise appearance.

Jill Dando 📺 (1988-99)
The shocking murder of Dando on her doorstep in 1999 remains unsolved.

Moira Stuart 📺 (1981-2007)
Peter Woods 📺 (1964-81)
Woods is the biological father of BBC journalist and presenter Justin Webb.

Nan Winton 📺 (1960-61)
Winton was the BBC's first on-screen female newsreader in a shortlived 1960 trial deemed unacceptable by viewers.

Reginald Bosanquet 📺 (1967-79)
Michael Aspel 📺 (1960-68)
Corbet Woodall 📺 (1963-67)
Anna Ford 📺 (1976-2006)
Jan Leeming 📺 (1980-87)
Lynette Lithgow 📺 (1988-96)
Selina Scott 📺 (1980-86)
Sue Lawley 📺 (1981-88)
Alongside her news duties, Lawley is best known for her 18-year stint presenting BBC Four's Desert Island Discs. She left the role in 2006.

Julia Somerville 📺 (1983-99)

Cars of the 1970s

How did you get around in the seventies? Was it in one of the decade's fancy new Range Rovers, or perhaps something more modest like a Morris Marina? Here are the decade's most famous (and infamous) cars.

Ford Capri

Vauxhall HC Viva

Ford Escort

Introduced in 1968, the Ford Escort went on to be the best-selling car in Britain in the 1980s and 1990s. The car was brought back into the spotlight in 2013, when it was featured in Fast & Furious 6.

Jaguar XJ

Triumph TR7

Austin Allegro

Austin Maxi

The Austin Maxi was the first British five-door hatchback, and one of the first cars to be featured on the BBC's Wheelbase show.

Ford Cortina

Ford Granada

Designed as a European executive car, the Granada was popular for taxi and police car use. It was also modified for use as a hearse and limousine, and was often seen in The Sweeney.

Leyland Princess

Triumph Dolomite

Vauxhall Cavalier

Range Rover

Morris Marina

The popular Morris Marina is ranked amongst the worst cars ever built. The car was released with poor suspension, chronic understeer, and windscreen wipers fitted the wrong way round.

Hillman Avenger

Saab 99

Datsun Sunny

BMW 316

Volkswagen Beetle

Affectionately known as the bug in English-speaking countries, it is called turtle in Bolivia, frog in Indonesia, and hunchback in Poland.

Household Goods in 1980

Mortgage interest rates were around 15% as we went into the eighties, not much lower as we left, and added to our basket in 1980. If you had any money left over perhaps you were spending it on home perms, cement and lamb's liver!

Lamb's liver

Tea bags
Tea is one of the few items included in the basket since the start. Tea bags were added in 1980; loose tea was removed in 2002.

Smash
Smash sales soared following the 1974 TV adverts featuring the Smash Martians. It was replaced in 1987 by oven chips.

Cider

Wine

Mortgage Interest

White spirit

Cement

Toilet seat

Electric plug

Colour TV
Colour TV sets outnumbered black and white sets in 1976.

Record player

Cassette recorder
Cassette recorders were first introduced by Philips in the 1960s and were originally intended for dictation and journalists.

Electric hairdryer

Carpet sweeper

Continental quilt

Drycell batteries

Colour photo film

Briefcase

Home perm

National Trust fees
Membership to the National Trust significantly increased throughout the 1980s (around 5.6 million people are members today). The Giant's Causeway is the most visited national attraction.

Olympic Medallists in Your Life

With seven gold medals, Jason Kenny is without equal while the unique achievements of Laura Trott – now Mrs Kenny – brings the household tally to twelve. Meanwhile, over at the Paralympics, swimmer-cyclist Sarah Storey has an incredible 17 gold medals. And medals of all colours? Here are the heroes of Team GB at the Summer Olympics.

Jason Kenny (9) 🥇 Cycling

Bradley Wiggins (8) 🥇 Cycling

Britain's most decorated Olympian until Kenny took the crown in Tokyo, Wiggo acquired various nicknames throughout his career. In France he was referred to as 'Le Gentleman', while the Dutch apparently called him 'The Banana with the Sideburns'.

Chris Hoy (7) 🥇 Cycling

Laura Kenny (6) 🥇 Cycling

Our most successful female Olympian with five gold medals, Trott (now Kenny) began life with a collapsed lung and asthma.

Steve Redgrave (6) 🥇 Rowing

Max Whitlock (6) 🥇 Gymnastics

Charlotte Dujardin (6) 🥇 Equestrianism

Ben Ainslie (5) 🥇 Sailing

Known for his hot temper, Ben Ainslie has accused competitors of teaming up against him. He was disqualified from the world championships in Australia for confronting a photographer who Ainslie felt had impeded his progress.

Adam Peaty (5) 🥇 Swimming

Katherine Grainger (5) 🥇 Rowing

Grainger is the first British woman to win medals at five successive Olympic games, from Sydney to Rio.

Mo Farah (4) 🥇 Athletics

Matthew Pinsent (4) 🥇 Rowing

Ed Clancy (4) 🥇 Cycling

Ian Stark (4) 🥇 Equestrianism

Louis Smith (4) 🥇 Gymnastics

Becky Adlington (4) 🥇 Swimming

Seb Coe (4) 🥇 Athletics

Ginny Leng (4) 🥇 Equestrianism

It's striking that our most decorated Olympians did so in recent decades. Of the 18 athletes earning four medals or more since you were born, Seb Coe came off the starting blocks first: he won his first medal at the 1980 Moscow Olympics at the age of 23 (shortly after breaking the 1,000 metre record in Oslo, above).

Run the slide rule over every modern Olympics, starting in 1896, and only six more GB athletes have achieved the same phenomenal success.

Winter Olympics Venues Since You Were Born

Unless you're an athlete or winter sports fan, the Winter Olympics can slip past almost unnoticed. These are the venues; can you remember the host countries and years?

Lillehammer
Salt Lake City
Sapporo
Albertville
The last Games to be held in the same year as the Summer Olympics, with the next Winter Olympics held two years later.

Turin
Grenoble
Sarajevo
Lake Placid
Sochi
Innsbruck (twice)
This usually snowy city experienced its mildest winter in 60 years; the army was called in to transport snow and ice from the mountains. Nevertheless, twelve years later, the Winter Olympics were back.

Nagano
Calgary
Vancouver
PyeongChang

Answers: *Lillehammer: Norway, 1994; Salt Lake City: USA, 2002; Sapporo: Japan, 1972; Albertville: France, 1992; Turin: Italy, 2006; Grenoble: France, 1968; Sarajevo: Yugoslavia, 1984; Lake Placid: USA, 1980; Sochi: Russia, 2014; Innsbruck: Austria, 1964; Nagano: Japan, 1998; Calgary: Canada, 1988; Innsbruck: Austria, 1976; Vancouver: Canada, 2010; PyeongChang: South Korea, 2018*

Fashion in the Eighties

Eighties fashion was many things, but subtle wasn't one of them. Brash influences were everywhere from aerobics to Wall Street, from pop princesses to preppy polo shirts. The result was chaotic, but fun. How many eighties throwbacks still lurk in your closet?

Shoulder pads or puffed sleeves

Scrunchies
Patented in 1987 by nightclub singer Rommy Revson, the first scrunchie was designed using the waistband of her pyjama bottoms. The softer alternative to hair bands was named after Revson's dog Scunchie (no, that's not a typo).

Conical bras
Inspired by 1950s bullet bras, Jean Paul Gaultier introduced the cone bra in 1984. As a child he fashioned the bra for his teddy bear; years later he reworked the look for Madonna's Blonde Ambition tour in 1990.

Acid wash jeans

Slogan t-shirts
Designer Katharine Hamnett introduced slogan t-shirts, famously revealing one displaying an anti-nuclear statement when meeting Margaret Thatcher in 1984. Wham opted for 'Choose Life'; for Frankie Goes to Hollywood it was 'Frankie Says Relax'.

Leotards and leg-warmers
Leg-warmers reached the masses following the release of Fame and Flashdance, as well as Jane Fonda exercise videos. Nowadays, leg-warmers are even worn by babies while they have their nappies changed.

Deely boppers, bangle earrings or a polka dot hair bow

Pedal pushers or leggings

Guyliner

Levi 501s

Pixie boots

Ra-ra skirt and PVC belts

Dr Martens
Dr Martens were designed by a German soldier to aid the recovery of his broken foot. Pete Townshend of The Who was the first rock star to wear the boots on stage, and the shoe was adopted by numerous subcultures.

Grand Designs

Governments around the world spent much of the 20th century nation building (and rebuilding). Here is a selection of striking civil engineering achievements between the ages of 0 and 40.

1962	Butlins, Minehead
1965	Mont Blanc Tunnel, France & Italy
1965	Zeeland Bridge, Netherlands
1966	**Almondsbury Interchange, Bristol & Gloucester** The Almondsbury Interchange was the first example of a four-level stack in the UK, and remains one of only three of its kind in the country.
1967	**Second Blackwall Tunnel, London** The second Blackwall tunnel is relatively straight, unlike the first which is curved. That was to avoid a sewer, but also reportedly so that horses (the main means of transport when built) didn't see daylight at the other end and bolt.
1969	Humber Refinery, Northern Lincolnshire
1970	Aswan Dam, Aswan
1970	Hyde Park Barracks, London
1971	**Spaghetti Junction, Birmingham** Officially the Gravelly Hill Interchange, Spaghetti Junction was named by the Guinness Book of World Records as 'the most complex interchange on the British road system'.
1973	Bosphorus Bridge, Istanbul
1976	**Sonnenberg Tunnel, Lucerne** A 5,000 ft road tunnel that was built to double up as a nuclear shelter for up to 20,000 people. Blast doors at the entrance weigh 350 tons...but take 24 hours to close.
1981	Humber Bridge, Kingston upon Hull
1982	Thames Barrier, London
1984	Kylesku Bridge, Scotland (Drochaid a' Chaolais Chumhaing)
1989	Grande Arche, Paris
1994	**Channel Tunnel, UK & France** The idea of a tunnel between the two countries goes back to the 1800s, and Napoleon supported the idea. The tunnel was recognised as one of the 'Seven Wonders of the Modern World' by the American Society of Civil Engineers.

World Buildings

Buildings that are known the world over for all the right (and the wrong) reasons and were opened before you turned 50.

968	Madison Square Garden, New York City, New York
969	John Hancock Center, Chicago
973	Sears Tower, Chicago, Illinois
973	World Trade Center, New York
973	**Sydney Opera House, Sydney** The estimated cost for the construction was AU$7m (£4m). It ended up costing AU$102m (£59m), and took 14 years to build rather than the four years planned.
976	CN Tower, Toronto
977	Pompidou Centre, Paris
981	Sydney Tower, Sydney
990	Washington National Cathedral, Washington DC
983	**Trump Tower, New York** How many floors there are in Trump Tower? An easy question, right? It was built with 58 floors. But Trump wasn't happy... the ceilings are high on some floors, so the numbers jump from the 6th to the 13th floor. Now it has 68!
988	Parliament House, Canberra
989	Louvre Pyramid, Paris
996	Petronas Twin Towers, Kuala Lampur
997	**Guggenheim Museum, Bilbao** Bilbao saw a surge in economic growth following the museum's opening. The 'Bilbao effect' is now the name for the positive local impact a building can instigate.
999	Burj Al Arab, Dubai
2000	Emirates Tower One, Dubai
2007	Heydar Aliyev Center, Baku
2008	Atlantis, The Palm, Dubai
2010	**Burj Khalifa, Dubai** At half a mile high, it's the world's tallest building and freestanding structure.

Household Goods in 1987

The shelves, fridges and freezers are piled high with convenience foods. What did we do with all that extra time we'd saved? First, dig out the indigestion tablets. Then tackle a spot of DIY and finally move house, it seems!

Squash racket
The classic eighties sport. Prince Philip played squash to relax while Queen Elizabeth II was in labour with Prince Charles.

Muesli

Spaghetti

Jam doughnuts

Swiss roll

Beefburgers

Mince

Garlic sausage

Frozen prawns

Brie

Red Leicester
Originally called Leicestershire Cheese, the cheese was renamed Red Leicester after World War II to differentiate it from 'White Leicester' made during rationing when the use of colouring agents was banned.

Conifer

Frozen curry and rice

Fish and chips
Synonymous with British cuisine and described by Winston Churchill as 'the good companions', fish and chips were exempt from rationing during World War II, as the government feared any limitations would damage the morale of the nation.

VHS recorder

Ready mixed filler

Home telephone
The popularity of mobile phones has led to a decrease of landlines. Only 73% of British households had a landline used to make calls in 2020.

Fabric conditioner

Estate agent fees

Indigestion tablets

Books of the Decade

By our forties, most of us have decided what we like to read. But occasionally a book can break the spell, revealing the delights of other genres. Did any of these newly published books do that for you?

2002	Everything Is Illuminated by Jonathan Safran Foer
2002	**The Lovely Bones by Alice Sebold**

At university, Sebold was beaten and sexually assaulted in a location where a girl had previously been murdered. Her experience and her subsequent reactions to it informed a novel called Monsters about the rape and murder of a teenager, later retitled as The Lovely Bones.

2003	The Kite Runner by Khaled Hosseini
2003	Vernon God Little by DBC Pierre
2003	Brick Lane by Monica Ali
2004	The Line of Beauty by Alan Hollinghurst
2004	Cloud Atlas by David Mitchell
2004	Gilead by Marilynne Robinson
2004	Small Island by Andrea Levy
2005	Never Let Me Go by Kazuo Ishiguro
2005	The Book Thief by Markus Zusak
2005	The Sea by John Banville
2005	**The Girl with the Dragon Tattoo by Stieg Larsson**

Larsson died before the first three books in the series were published. Larsson's partner has a partially completed fourth book – but not the rights to publish it.

2005	Saturday by Ian McEwan
2006	The Road by Cormac McCarthy
2007	A Thousand Splendid Suns by Khaled Hosseini
2007	The Ghost by Robert Harris
2008	The White Tiger by Aravind Adiga
2008	The Hunger Games by Suzanne Collins
2009	Wolf Hall by Hilary Mantel
2009	The Help by Kathryn Stockett
2010	The Hand That First Held Mine by Maggie O'Farrell
2010	The Finkler Question by Howard Jacobson
2011	Fifty Shades of Grey by EL James
2011	A Dance with Dragons by George RR Martin

US Vice Presidents in Your Lifetime

The linchpin of a successful presidency, a springboard to become POTUS, or both? Here are the men – and the woman – who have shadowed the most powerful person in the world in your lifetime. (President in brackets.)

1961–63	Lyndon B Johnson (John F Kennedy)
1965–69	**Hubert Humphrey** (Lyndon Johnson) Christmas 1977: with just weeks to live, the former VP made goodbye calls. One was to Richard Nixon, the man who had beaten Humphrey to become president in 1968. Sensing Nixon's unhappiness at his status as Washington outcast, Humphrey invited him to take a place of honour at the funeral he knew was fast approaching.
1969–73	**Spiro Agnew (right)**
1973–74	Gerald Ford
1974–77	Nelson Rockefeller
1977–81	Walter Mondale
1981–89	**George HW Bush** He is only the second vice president to win the presidency while holding the office of vice president.
1989–93	**Dan Quayle** You say potato, Quayle said potatoe: he famously told a student to add an 'e' during a 1992 school visit.
1993–2001	**Al Gore** Gore won the Nobel Peace Prize in 2007. Two others have won: Teddy Roosevelt (1906) and Charles Dawes (1925).
2001–09	Dick Cheney
2009–17	Joe Biden
2017–20	**Mike Pence** In the 90s, Pence took a break from politics to become a conservative radio talk show and television host.
2020–	**Kamala Harris** Harris is the highest-ranked woman in US history and the first woman of colour to hold the office of Vice President. 'While I may be the first woman in this office, I will not be the last,' she said.

Spiro Agnew resigned in 1973, the second VP to quit in America's history (the first was John Calhoun in 1932). He stepped down after being charged with tax evasion and taking bribes. He covered his legal debts with a loan from friend Frank Sinatra. In 1983, Agnew was compelled to repay $268,000: the money he had taken in bribes, plus interest.

Stamps in the Seventies

By the seventies, any hobbyist intent on keeping a complete ongoing collection needed deep pockets (or a rich uncle). New stamps were churned out several times a year and the subjects became ever more esoteric: not just flowers and trees but racket sports, or paintings of horse races. Was your album gathering dust by then?

1970	Commonwealth Games
1971	British rural architecture
1972	Polar explorers
1972	Village churches
1972	Royal Silver Wedding celebration
1973	Plant a Tree Year
1973	County Cricket
1973	**400th anniversary of the birth of Inigo Jones** Not a household name by today's standards, Jones was an early and influential architect. He designed Covent Garden Square and parts of St Paul's Cathedral.
1973	Royal Wedding (Princess Anne and Mark Phillips)
1973	Britain's entry into the EC
1974	Medieval Warriors
1975	Sailing
1975	100 years since the birth of Jane Austen
1976	100 years of the telephone
1976	**British cultural traditions** The four chosen were a Morris dancer, a Scots piper, a Welsh harpist and an Archdruid.
1977	Racket sports
1977	Silver Jubilee
1977	Wildlife
1978	**Energy resources** In an era before renewable energy the choices made were oil, coal, natural gas and electricity.
1978	Horses
1979	Dogs
1979	Spring wild flowers
1979	Paintings of horse races
1979	150 years of the Metropolitan Police

More Things People Do Now...

... that nobody ever did when you were small – because
they couldn't, wouldn't, or definitely shouldn't!

- **Place a bet *during* a sporting event**
  This became popular in the 1990s; first on the phone, now online.

- Turn on underfloor heating

- **Buy soft toilet rolls**
  In 1942, a wonder was created in Walthamstow's St Andrews Road,
  one for which the bottoms of the world owe a huge debt: two-ply,
  soft toilet roll ('It's splinter-free'!). It was christened Andrex.

- Talk to a smart speaker

- Clean up dog poo (not doing it has been an offence since 1996)

- Listen to a podcast

- **Do a Sudoku puzzle**
  How many Japanese words do you know? Tsunami? Karaoke?
  Sake? In 2005, you likely added another: Sudoku (meaning
  'single number'). The puzzle originated in the USA – but was
  popularised by Wayne Gould, a Hong Kong judge from New
  Zealand who found a translated version in a Tokyo bookshop.

- **Cheat in a pub quiz**
  Which two capital cities mean the same in different languages?
  Who knows? Google knows, and a quick trip to the loo (phone
  in hand) is a modern phenomenon. (The answer is Sierra Leone's
  Freetown and Gabon's Libreville – but of course you knew that.)

- Order something for same day delivery

- Use chopsticks

- Fly a drone

- **Never watch live TV**
  Owning a TV but not watching any live programmes (just
  streamed content) might sound odd. But that is the reality for
  many – and around 1.5m have ditched the TV completely.

- Eat in the street

- Buy water

- **Use SatNav**
  In the 1980s, Ronald Reagan permitted civilian use of satellites
  for navigation and opened up a world in which we never need to
  get lost again – unless we want to. Or the USA pulls the plug.

- Argue for hours with strangers you'll never meet

A Lifetime of Progress

It's easy to lose sight of the breadth and pace of life-enhancing inventions made as you grew up – although some of these didn't stand the test of time! These are the biggies before you turned 50.

1988	**Internet virus** The first Internet worm (ie self-replicating) was designed to go after passwords. Its inventor was the son of the man who invented… computer passwords.
1989	World Wide Web
1990	Hubble space telescope
1991	Websites
1992	Digital hand-sized mobile phone
1994	Bluetooth
1995	**Mouse with scroll wheel** Mouse scroll wheels were developed for large Excel sheets but soon became used as a means of scrolling any content.
1996	DVD player
1997	WebTV
1998	Google
1999	Wi-Fi
2000	Camera phone
2001	**Wikipedia** Initially intended to be written by experts, around two dozen articles were written in the first year, so Wikipedia was opened up for anyone to edit. Around 5 million articles in English now await the curious, with many more in languages from Swedish to Tagalog. Little surprise that one article is a list of lists of lists.
2004	Facebook
2007	**Apple iPhone** The top-secret development of the iPhone began in 2004 under the code name 'Project Purple'. It was announced at a convention by Steve Jobs in 2007 at 9:41am; that's why iPhone adverts show the time 09:41 on the phones.
2009	**Bitcoin** Bitcoin mining (creating new bitcoins and checking transactions) uses as much as energy as all the USA's fridge

FA Cup Winners
Since You Were Born

Many fans have waited decades to see their team lift the cup; many more are still waiting. Here are the teams that have hoisted the trophy in your lifetime (last win in brackets).

West Bromwich Albion ⚽ (1967-68)
Leeds United ⚽ (1971-72)
Sunderland ⚽ (1972-73)
Southampton ⚽ (1975-76)
Ipswich Town ⚽ (1977-78)
West Ham United ⚽ (1979-80)
Coventry City ⚽ (1986-87)
Wimbledon ⚽ (1987-88)
Wimbledon shocked the country in 1988 when they beat First Division champions Liverpool in the FA Cup final, overcoming 17-1 odds.

Tottenham Hotspur ⚽ (1990-91)
Everton ⚽ (1994-95)
Liverpool ⚽ (2005-06)
Steven Gerrard made FA Cup history during the 2006 final against West Ham, scoring a thunderous 30-yard strike to take the game to extra time.

Portsmouth ⚽ (2007-08)
Wigan Athletic ⚽ (2012-13)
Manchester United ⚽ (2015-16)
Chelsea ⚽ (2017-18)
Former Chelsea and Ivory Coast striker Didier Drogba is the only player to score in four separate FA Cup Finals.

Manchester City ⚽ (2018-19)
Arsenal ⚽ (2019-20)
Leicester City ⚽ (2020-21)
The Foxes first FA Cup was a long time coming – as was their first triumph in the Premier League, achieved in 2015/16. Faithful fans who laid bets at 5,000 to 1 at the start of that season were richly rewarded; others did the same but cashed out early, enticed by the bookies.

Gameshow Hosts of the Seventies and Eighties

What do points make? I've started so I'll finish. Shut that door! You can't beat a bit of Bully! The catchphrases echo down the ages from these much-loved TV favourites.

David Vine ➤ (A Question of Sport)
Stuart Hall ➤ (It's a Knockout)
Anneka Rice ➤ (Treasure Hunt)
Kenneth Kendall ➤ (Treasure Hunt)
Cilla Black ➤ (Blind Date)
Born Priscilla White, the stage name of Cilla Black came about by mistake. Featured in the first issue of Mersey Beat newspaper, the journalist accidentally called her Cilla Black. Cilla liked the name and opted to keep it.

Barry Cryer ➤ (Jokers Wild)
Nicholas Parsons ➤ (Just a Minute, Sale of the Century)
Jim Bowen ➤ (Bullseye)
After completing his national service in the bomb disposal unit, Jim Bowen worked as a teacher and was promoted to deputy head, but gave up teaching once he appeared on The Comedians alongside Mike Reid.

Mike Read ➤ (Pop Quiz)
David Coleman ➤ (A Question of Sport)
Prof. Heinz Wolff ➤ (The Great Egg Race)
Bob Holness ➤ (Blockbusters)
Magnus Magnusson ➤ (Mastermind)
Angela Rippon ➤ (Masterteam)
Noel Edmonds ➤ (Telly Addicts)
Noel Edmonds has made headlines for plotting to buy the BBC, starting a pet counselling service, and driving a mannequin called Candice around in his black cab to dissuade the public from trying to flag him down.

Ted Rogers ➤ (3-2-1)
Terry Wogan ➤ (Blankety Blank)
Les Dawson ➤ (Blankety Blank)
Larry Grayson ➤ (The Generation Game)

Popular Food in the 1980s

Our last trolley dash takes us down the aisle at lunchtime, piled high with eat-on-the-go snacks and sandwiches. Stop on the way home for a deep pan pizza and a Diet Coke; end the day with a slice of Battenberg cake. Congratulations, you've just eaten the eighties!

Crunchy Nut Cornflakes
The cereal was invented in Manchester in 1980. Pity the poor Americans: it took 30 years for Crunchy Nut to cross the Atlantic.

Kellogg's Fruit and Fibre
Prepacked sandwiches
The prepacked sandwich was first sold by M&S in spring 1980. The range was small, conservative, made in-store and used whatever ingredients were plentiful (even if that was pilchards).

Viennetta
Trifle
In 1596, Thomas Dawson recorded the first recipe for trifle in his books, *The Good Huswifes Jewell*. It was essentially thick cream, rosewater, sugar and ginger. Jelly didn't appear until the 1700s.

Chicken Kiev

Vol au vent

Battenberg cake
Pizza
Pizza Hut claim to be the first company to sell food online - one of their signature pizzas via their Pizanet website, back in 1994.

Garlic bread

Kiwi

Sun-dried tomatoes

Potato waffles

Happy Meals
Diet Coke
Within two years of its unveiling in 1982, Diet Coke became the most popular diet soft drink in the world, and the third most popular soft drink overall behind Coca Cola and Pepsi.

Rowntree's Drifters

Hedgehog-flavoured crisps

Burton's fish 'n' chips

Chicken satay

Eighties Symbols of Success

In the flamboyant era of Dallas and Dynasty there were many ways to show that you, too, had really made it. Forty years on, it's fascinating to see how some of these throwbacks are outdated or available to nearly everyone, while others are still reserved for today's wealthy peacocks.

Car phone
Dishwasher
Children at private school
Waterbed
The modern-day waterbed was designed by a US student for his master's thesis project. Original fillings included corn syrup, and then jelly, before he settled on water. They were popular but problematic due to their weight and susceptibility to puncture, as Edward Scissorhands found out.

Second cars
Holidays abroad
Conservatory
Pony
Colour TV
Diamonds
Cordless phone
Birkin bag
A chance encounter between Hermès Executive Chairman Jean-Louis Dumas and Jane Birkin on a plane inspired the Birkin bag. The contents of Birkin's bag spilled out, and Dumas suggested she needed a bag with pockets, so Birkin sketched her idea on a sick bag.

Double glazing
Rolex watch
Leather Filofax
Mont Blanc pen
Newton's Cradle desk toy
Named after Isaac Newton and the cat's cradle, an early version was wooden, expensive and sold at Harrods. Chrome imitations followed. TV programme Myth Busters built a supersized cradle with concrete-filled chrome wrecking balls... it didn't work.

Stone cladding

The first UK car phone call was made in 1959 from outside the Lymm Hotel in Cheshire; human operators were used to connect calls until the 1980s. John Lennon wrote the lyrics for I'm Only Sleeping on the back of a car phone demand letter.

Cars of the 1980s

Many cars you might associate with the eighties were on the road long before then, from the Ford Granada and Escort to the Porsche 911. But this is the decade they arguably hit their stride alongside other automotive icons.

Toyota Corolla
Introduced in 1966, the Toyota Corolla became the best-selling car worldwide by 1974. The car was named after a ring of petals.

Volvo 240

BMW 3 Series

Volkswagen Golf
Sold as the Rabbit in the US and the Caribe in Mexico.

Volkswagen Passat

Vauxhall Astra

Triumph Acclaim

Porsche 911
Originally the Porsche 901 on its 1964 debut, the name was changed after Peugeot claimed they had exclusive rights to naming cars with three digits and a zero in the middle.

Jaguar XJS

Nissan Micra

Peugeot 205

Austin Maestro

Vauxhall Nova
The Vauxhall Nova inspired a series of comical bumper stickers, including 'You've been Novataken', and 'Vauxhall Casanova'. It was called the Corsa everywhere but Britain where it sounded too much like the word 'coarser'. It was renamed anyway in 1993.

Ford Sierra
Neil Kinnock had one of the first Sierras. He wrecked it in a crash.

Austin Montego

Volkswagen Polo

Austin Metro
Promoted with comical adverts, the car became one of the best-selling cars in UK history, and even Princess Diana owned one.

Ford Fiesta
The Fiesta is the UK's best-selling car of all time.

Vauxhall Cavalier

Eighties TV Gameshows

By the eighties, new formats aimed at youngsters - your youngsters? - were introduced. Some shows went digital or took to the skies; others kept it (very) simple, and a few remain family favourites to this day.

The Adventure Game

Treasure Hunt

Blind Date

The pilot episode of Blind Date was hosted by Duncan Norvelle, but he was quickly replaced by Cilla Black. Black presented the entire original run of the series for eighteen years, before unexpectedly announcing her departure on the show's first ever live episode.

Surprise Surprise

Countdown

Catchphrase

Blockbusters

Telly Addicts

3-2-1

The show's mascot and booby prize, Dusty Bin, cost around £10,000 to build. He was built by visual effects engineer Ian Rowley, who also operated Dusty Bin in the studio.

Blankety Blank

Bob's Full House

The instantly recognisable scoreboard was dubbed Mr Babbage by original host Bob Monkhouse. This was a nod to Charles Babbage, the inventor of the first programmable computer. In the reboot, Mr Babbage was replaced with a colour scoreboard, but the original board soon returned.

Bullseye

Cheggers Plays Pop

Family Fortunes

The Great Egg Race

Give Us a Clue

The Krypton Factor

Play Your Cards Right

The Price is Right

The Pyramid Game

Popular Boys' Names

58

The most favoured names are now a curious blend of the evergreen (Thomas), the rediscovered (Harry), and those enjoying their first proper outing (Joshua).

Oliver
George
Arthur
Noah
Muhammad
Leo
Oscar
Harry
Archie
Jack

Of the top ten names above, Noah, Harry and Jack are falling; all the others have never been more popular than they are now.

Henry
Charlie
Freddie
Theodore
Thomas
Finley
Theo
Alfie
Jacob
William
Isaac
Tommy
Joshua
James
Lucas
Alexander
Arlo
Roman

Rising stars:
Milo, Yusuf, Otis and Myles all make their first appearance in the most popular names of 2020.

Books of the Decade

Our final decade of books are the bookstore favourites from your fifties. How many did you read...and can you remember the plot, or the cover?

012	**Gone Girl by Gillian Flynn** Many believed that Gone Girl drew inspiration from the real life disappearance and murder of Laci Peterson. While Flynn acknowledged the similarities, she stated that this was untrue and the story was influenced by her fondness for Who's Afraid of Virginia Woolf.
013	Doctor Sleep by Stephen King
014	Big Little Lies by Liane Moriarty
015	**The Girl on the Train by Paula Hawkins** The use of the word 'girl' in the title of the book sparked debate upon its release. It was speculated that it was used to liken it to Gone Girl, but it was used in the working title long before Hawkins had read Gone Girl.
016	Dark Matter by Blake Crouch
017	Little Fires Everywhere by Celeste Ng
018	Where the Crawdads Sing by Delia Owens
018	**The Outsider by Stephen King** It's not unusual to see a character from one Stephen King novel appear in another. Before appearing in The Outsider, Holly Gibney had been a part of the Bill Hodges trilogy, and later the main character in If It Bleeds.
019	The Beekeeper of Aleppo by Christy Lefteri
019	**The Silent Patient by Alex Michaelides** As a disillusioned screenwriter, Michaelides wrote a novel which became The Silent Patient. The story was inspired by the Greek heroine Alcestis.
020	The Vanishing Half by Brit Bennett
020	The Midnight Library by Matt Haig
020	The Thursday Murder Club by Richard Osman
020	Hamnet by Maggie O'Farrell
021	The Wife Upstairs by Rachel Hawkins
021	Beautiful World, Where Are You by Sally Rooney

April 17 1970: Jim Lovell is brought aboard a helicopter, the last of the three astronauts from the Apollo 13 mission to be lifted from the floating

Apollo Astronauts

Of those who have been to the moon, twelve landed, twelve remained in orbit. Gus Grissom, Ed White, and Roger B Chaffee died in training. BBC and ITV broadcast the June 1969 landing live in the first all-night transmission. Touchdown was at 9.17pm UK time – past your bedtime? – but Armstrong didn't take his monumental step until 3.56am.

Landed on the moon:

Alan Bean

Alan Shepard

Shepard was the oldest person to walk on the moon at the age of 47.

Buzz Aldrin

Charles Duke

David Scott

Edgar Mitchell

Eugene Cernan

Harrison Schmitt

James Irwin

John Young

Neil Armstrong

Pete Conrad

Remained in low orbit:

Al Worden

Bill Anders

Anders took the iconic Earthrise photo.

Dick Gordon

Frank Borman

Fred Haise

Jack Swigert

Jim Lovell

Ken Mattingly

Michael Collins

Ron Evans

Made the final spacewalk of the program to retrieve film cassettes.

Stuart Roosa

On the Apollo 14 mission he carried seeds from 5 species of trees. They were planted across the US and are known as Moon Trees.

Tom Stafford

Popular Girls' Names

Of the fifty names that made the Top 10 from 1900-74, only four have appeared since: Claire, Emma, Samantha and Sarah. (Oddly, names beginning with 'D' are now a rarity with no Top 10 entries in the last fifty years!)

Olivia

Along with other names ending in 'a' - look at the top five names here! - Olivia rose to popularity in the late nineties and has remained a favourite ever since. She's been number one or two from 2008 to the present day.

Amelia
Isla
Ava
Mia
Ivy
Lily
Isabella
Rosie
Sophia
Grace
Freya
Willow
Florence
Emily
Ella
Poppy
Evie
Elsie
Charlotte
Evelyn
Sienna
Sofia
Daisy
Phoebe
Sophie

Rising stars:

Myla, Lyra, Elodie and Eden are new, alongside Maeve - she's the on/off love interest of new boy Otis in a hit Netflix series!

Things People Did When You Were Growing Up (Part 2)

Finally, here are more of the things we saw, we did and errands we ran as kids that nobody needs, wants, or even understands how to do in the modern age!

Drink syrup of figs

Preserve vegetables

Save the silver chocolate papers from Roses

Eat offal
Tripe was never on ration but long out of favour by the time the tripe dresser's fate was sealed in 1992, when BSE broke out.

Make a carbon copy
Carbon paper was first patented by Ralph Wedgwood, son of Thomas Wedgwood, in 1806, for his Noctograph – designed to help blind people write without ink. The smell and texture are just a memory, but emails sent in 'cc' (carbon copy) might remind you!

Wash handkerchiefs
You'd have to keep (and wash) a hanky for nine years to outweigh the CO_2 emissions of its tissue cousins.

Use talcum powder

Make a penfriend

Wire a plug
Strip and route wires to the terminal; fit the right fuse. Not any more. In 1994, it became illegal to sell appliances without fitted plugs.

Darn a hole in your sock

Refill your pen from an inkwell

Wind on your camera for another shot

See the bones in your foot at the shoe shop through a Pedoscope

Pluck a chicken

Smoke on a bus
'When will this fanaticism going to stop?' asked one MP in 1962, about a proposed ban on lower-deck smoking.

Scrape ice patterns off the inside of your bedroom window

Service your own car

Buy starch or blue bags for your washing

Play Spot the Ball
Spot the Ball was launched in 1973. More than 10 years passed without a jackpot winner as its popularity declined.

Printed in Great Britain
by Amazon